The Right Fit

Recruiting, Selecting, and Orienting Staff

Kay Albrecht

NEW HORIZONS

EDUCATIONAL CONSULTANTS AND LEARNING RESOURCES

LAKE FOREST, ILLINOIS 60045-0863

Printed in the United States of America

Library of Congress Cataloging-in-Publication Data

Albrecht, Kay M.
    The right fit recruiting, selecting, and orienting
staff / Kay Albrecht. — 1st ed.
    p. cm. – (The director's toolbox)
    Includes bibliographical references.
    ISBN 0-9621894-6-4

    1. School employees—Selection and appointment.
2. Early childhood education—Administration. 3. School
personnel management. I. Title. II. Series.

LB2831.57.545A43 2002   372.21'0683
                        QBI02-200784

NEW HORIZONS

Educational Consultants and Learning Resources
P.O. Box 863
Lake Forest, Illinois 60045-0863
(847) 295-8131
(847) 295-2968 FAX

Books in **The Director's Toolbox Management Series** are available at quantity discounts for use in training programs. For information on bulk quantity rates or how to purchase a **Trainer's Guide** for this book, contact the publisher.

Illustrations – Marc Bermann

Design – Stan Burkat

Editor – Paula Jorde Bloom

CONTENTS

Chapter

About the Author

Kay Albrecht is on the staff of *Innovations in Early Childhood Education* in Houston, Texas. She received her undergraduate degree from the University of Louisiana at Lafayette and her master's degree and doctorate from the University of Tennessee at Knoxville. A former teacher of young children and director of an accredited center, Dr. Albrecht has held academic appointments at four universities. She is a frequent contributor to *Child Care Information Exchange*, serves as a consultant on special projects, and works internationally with Exchange as the academic dean of the World Forum on Early Care and Education. Kay is the author of numerous articles and the *Innovations* series of books on infant, toddler, and preschool development, curriculum, and training published by Gryphon House. This is her first book for New Horizons.

Acknowledgements

Many of the lessons about recruiting, selecting, and orienting teachers I learned from the talented professionals with whom I was privileged to work over the years at HeartsHome Early Learning Center, a nationally accredited program in Houston, Texas. Together we figured out where we were making mistakes and which new techniques or strategies to try. These teachers have my gratitude for helping me understand the recruitment, selection, and orientation process.

I am also grateful to Paula Jorde Bloom for mentoring me in the process of writing this book—I needed and appreciated her help and support. Appreciation is also extended to Teri Talan and Cara Levinson for their helpful feedback and to Catherine Cauman for the careful editing.

CHAPTER 1

Why Is It So Hard To Find Good Teachers?

You've just finished giving a prospective parent a tour of your center when one of your teachers approaches you and asks if she can talk with you later in the day. Your stomach sinks, your heart rate increases, your anxiety rises. After a quick run through a litany of possible reasons why she might want to talk with you, you settle on the one reason that strikes fear in your heart— she has decided to quit her job. Whether it is promotion to a new position, a family move, or dissatisfaction with some aspect of her work, the challenging task of recruiting a new teacher looms on your horizon.

When I talk with directors about the difficult parts of their job, finding good teachers always comes up. My own experience includes waking up frantic in the middle of the night wondering how I would find a replacement for a departing teacher who is competent and well liked by parents and peers. Directors know from experience that turnover, even when it is anticipated and planned, is costly. Sometimes we can't identify or quantify the costs, but we feel the cost of turnover in our workloads, the morale of teachers, and the never-ending challenge of staffing classrooms.

Much of the difficulty of recruitment is a result of the context of early care and education and the lack of adequate infrastructure to support and sustain our work. Another reason recruitment is so hard is that turnover has many costs, costs that are easy to see as well as those that are not as readily apparent.

The Context of Early Care and Education

As important as the work of early childhood education is to the future of children and families, our field faces many challenges and problems. Inadequate infrastructure in early care and education contributes to the difficulty of finding and keeping highly trained teachers. Let's look at a few of the contextual issues that impact the current staffing crisis.

Compensation levels are inadequate. No director has to be told about the issues relating to compensation. The link between overall compensation levels in the field and the ability to attract a pool of highly educated individuals for teaching positions is obvious. Salaries have stagnated at near-poverty levels. Teachers of young children earn half as much as comparably educated women and less than one-third as much as comparably educated men. The average salary for child care teachers in the United States is less than $20,000 annually—that's less than toll booth attendants, bellhops, or postal clerks. Many states report salaries below this average, particularly for teacher assistants and those who enter the profession without formal early childhood education training.

Reprinted with permission.

Low wages have plagued the field of early childhood for decades and have made the recruitment process for administrators particularly challenging. Many factors have contributed to this dismal picture—the robust economy during the 1990s, low unemployment, inadequate federal subsidies, and labor shortages in other female-dominated fields. Regardless of the reasons, employment opportunities available in other fields that pay better wages have decreased the pool of available applicants for early childhood positions. Qualified individuals simply go elsewhere for employment. They choose not to teach, or when they do teach, they take positions in publicly funded programs where salaries are somewhat higher than those in programs relying on parent fees.

The benefits picture is equally discouraging. Few teachers receive job benefits such as paid health insurance, vacation, and sick leave. Most teachers are without the basic benefits considered routine to workers in other professions.

Research conducted by the Center for the Child Care Workforce and the Center for Early Childhood Leadership has found that less than one-half of teachers working in programs funded by parent fees even receive health coverage.

Low morale, stress, and job burnout are prevalent. Educating young children is a job that is physically demanding, intellectually challenging, and involves a combination of routine and novel tasks and responsibilities. As a result, teachers often experience work overload with the unpleasant results of low morale and burnout. Low morale is contagious. If one staff member feels stressed and burned out, others are likely to share those feelings. The working conditions in many early childhood programs contribute to low morale and stress. Many caregivers endure hardships daily that make them question their long-term commitment to the field, even when they derive great satisfaction from working directly with children.

Professional status is low. Complicated by a view of child care as women's work, the general public devalues the contributions of all teachers, particularly those who work with children before they begin elementary school. The impact of status is seen in the overall decrease in students entering the teaching profession. As diverse career opportunities have increased, particularly for women, fewer college students are choosing to pursue teaching careers. Status is further compromised by poor compensation. When low status is combined with inadequate compensation, the attractiveness of the profession as a career choice declines even further.

Recruitment and selection strategies are often haphazard. A reality of staffing early childhood programs is that the work won't wait—an appropriate number of adults must be present to meet the needs of children, state and federal requirements, and accreditation criteria. As a result, the process of selecting staff is often inadequate. Called the warm-body syndrome by directors, the urgent need to fill a vacant position is often the driving force in the staff selection process. Recruitment that does not find the right fit between the center, the teacher, and the program is destined to fail and often creates a cycle of repeated turnover. Further, directors inadvertently increase teachers' stress as they struggle to staff programs.

Poor hiring decisions contribute to staff turnover. When the warm-body syndrome prevails as a hiring strategy, decisions about new hires are often made on the basis of who can start work at the optimum time rather than who is best suited and qualified for the position. In addition, directors often hire for now—planning to continue to look for a better candidate later. The lack of a match between the employee and the employer virtually guarantees that the new teacher will not succeed.

C hild care workers are at the receiving end of our national ambivalence toward child care.

Lilian Katz

Recruitment expectations are often unrealistic. Inadequate recruitment and selection are exacerbated by unrealistic expectations regarding resignations. Many centers request the standard two-week notice common in the business community. This short notice unwittingly creates the expectation that replacing teachers takes only two weeks. In reality, the process of recruitment often takes much longer.

When a new teacher is finally selected, there is a tendency to expect too much. Even experienced, credentialed teachers need time to assimilate into the culture of the new setting and figure out how things work. When new teachers are placed directly in the classroom without adequate orientation and pre-service training, the chances of successful integration decrease.

There are not enough teachers to fill vacant positions. Projections based on statistics of young children in out-of-home care indicate that more than two million infant, toddler, and preschool teachers and caregivers are needed to staff programs at the child/staff ratios recommended by the National Association for the Education of Young Children. The Department of Labor Statistics reports that there were less than a million teachers in early care and education settings in 2001. The discrepancy between the need and the available workforce is obvious. It also suggests that many classrooms are not staffed at recommended levels, increasing the chances of burnout, low morale, and compromised program quality.

There are not enough early childhood teacher preparation programs. As a director, you know that a well-trained staff is the key determinant of program quality and healthy child development. You also know that there are too few well-trained teachers available for hire. Applicants with the desired educational backgrounds are simply not available in adequate numbers.

When directors do find teachers with the right dispositions for early education, it is often difficult to find and provide appropriate training and educational resources to foster their professional development. Directors are faced with a professional development landscape where both traditional programs in community colleges and universities and training programs provided by local, state, and national organizations are inadequate to meet the professional development needs of their staff.

What Issues Impact You?

With this brief overview as a backdrop, take a moment to reflect on the infrastructure issues that impact you and your center. Read through the 12 issues in Exercise 1 and check those that reflect your current situation. The issues that impact your program provide clues as to how you can begin to design effective strategies to reduce the incidence of poor hiring decisions and unwanted turnover.

❑ The salaries I can offer teachers are not competitive with those of other jobs they might consider in the community.

❑ The benefits I can offer are insufficient to attract high-quality teachers.

❑ Low morale, job stress, and burnout among staff have been a problem.

❑ Teachers often complain about their low professional status.

❑ I am often caught off guard when a teacher resigns.

❑ Teachers comment on the work overload caused by turnover.

❑ The resignation notice period at my center does not allow enough time to find a replacement.

❑ I have been guilty of hiring a warm body to fill a position—someone without the desired qualifications.

❑ I have made more than my share of poor hiring decisions.

❑ Some staff I've hired have unrealistic expectations when they start their jobs.

❑ I can't find enough good applicants with the right credentials.

❑ There are not enough affordable teacher preparation programs in my community.

The High Cost of Turnover

How much does turnover cost? Although long considered an important issue in the business community, the direct and indirect costs of turnover in the early childhood arena have only recently been understood. Research conducted by the Center for the Child Care Workforce and other groups has revealed the implications of high turnover for children's development and the overall quality of program services. Direct replacement costs to fill positions, lost enrollment due to inadequate staffing, declining staff morale, family dissatisfaction, and negative outcomes for children's growth and development are a few of the consequences. They remind us that turnover is not a trivial matter; it is a serious issue demanding our attention.

Direct replacement costs. Staff turnover results in direct costs—costs that represent direct expenditures of funds. Direct costs can run from several hundred dollars per employee to several thousand. Direct costs include advertising, substitutes, telephone charges, criminal background checks, and postage, as well as the costs associated with orienting a new person to your program.

Lost enrollment. When turnover occurs, some families experience a breach of trust in the program, causing them to consider other options or leave the program entirely. Lost enrollment strains already tight budgets and makes programs financially vulnerable. These programs are more likely to close their doors than those that limit turnover while stabilizing enrollment revenues.

Lowered staff morale. One of the most unfortunate consequences of turnover for many programs is lowered teacher morale. Teachers who remain with the program often feel a sense of abandonment similar to the feelings of children who lose a teacher. They lose a connection, a colleague, and often a valued friend. They may consider other opportunities or different jobs. In addition, teachers who stay often face increased demands managing classroom routines, curriculum planning, and supervision responsibilities because of decreased staffing resources. This adds further to job stress and potentially to job dissatisfaction.

Increased parental stress. In addition to the stress placed on center staff, turnover can certainly increase stress on the families enrolled in your program. For some families, turnover triggers concerns about overall program operations. Parents may feel like their needs have not been considered in the change process, particularly if it was their child's teacher who departed.

It takes time to cultivate a trusting relationship with a caregiver. For some parents the disruption of that bond can be unsettling. A family may need to reorganize to accommodate the change. For many families this increases uncertainty and results in hypervigilance during the transition. The result may be closer scrutiny and an elevated concern about almost every detail of your program's operation. A lost sock or a child's rocky transition from home to school can turn into an upsetting episode and cause for concern.

Missed opportunities. Missed opportunities are another cost of turnover. Many regular job responsibilities in the center don't get done as you and your staff rearrange schedules to deal with the impact of a vacancy. Time spent screening and interviewing candidates means time away from other job-related tasks. Networking meetings missed and cancelled attendance at professional development conferences are real-life examples of missed opportunities.

Negative consequences for children. Considerable research confirms that children are affected by staff turnover. Changes in teachers create feelings of loss in children. When these feelings dominate a child's experience, the loss can trigger regression, behavior changes, and interrupted developmental progress. Research on this important subject has helped us understand that children who repeatedly experience high turnover of their primary caregiver engage in less social play and show less age-appropriate play behaviors. They also spend more time wandering aimlessly and develop vocabulary more slowly.

Increased administrative workload. Directors report that dealing with turnover is one of the most challenging dimensions of their job. Schedules and classroom assignments must be rearranged, more parent conferences and staff discussions need to be held, substitutes must be recruited and oriented, and the enrollment of new children may be delayed until vacancies are filled. Directors may find themselves substituting in the classroom to ensure adequate ratios. Everything changes when turnover occurs. Rather than dealing with the full range of tasks needed to accomplish their jobs, directors focus only on the recruitment process, seeking to fill vacant positions before they lose control of costs, children, families, teachers, and sometimes their own feelings of competence. This change in focus suspends other activities until the staffing problem is solved.

What Is the Impact of Turnover on Your Center?

Think about the consequences of turnover for your program as you complete Exercise 2. Next to each category, note the direct and indirect costs associated with turnover that you have experienced during the past year. Provide specific examples of the impact of staff departures on your program. Some costs are readily quantifiable (for example, dollars spent on advertising, time devoted to screening and interviewing candidates). Other consequences are less concrete (for example, staff grumbling about the extra workload, classroom management problems resulting from inexperienced substitutes).

exercise 2

Category	Examples
Direct replacement costs	
Lost enrollment	
Lowered staff morale	
Increased parental stress	
Missed opportunities	
Negative consequences for children	
Increased administrative workload	

Choosing a Different Model

It is possible to take control of the recruitment process and reduce the negative impact of turnover on everyone. In this book, you'll learn about implementing management strategies to improve your chances of being ready to recruit, screen, interview, and select replacements when vacancies occur. **The Right Fit** is both a philosophy and a set of strategies to help you think about this vital part of your administrative role in a more comprehensive way. The model includes five components:

- establishing systems so that recruitment is a continuous process
- determining the right fit between applicants and your program
- standardizing interviewing and screening procedures
- selecting the right candidate from the pool of applicants
- orienting new hires right from the start

Implementing the right fit model won't change the context of early care and education—the compensation and status issues that plague our field are far bigger than your program alone. It can, however, help ensure that you increase your chances of attracting the most qualified candidates available and reduce the likelihood of unwanted turnover and stress associated with the recruitment and screening process.

CHAPTER 2

Thinking about Recruitment as a Continuous Process

Stemming the incidence of high turnover and of being caught off guard by surprise resignations begins with adopting a new way of thinking about the recruitment and hiring processes at your center. It means shifting paradigms from thinking of recruitment as an isolated event or activity to thinking about recruitment as an ongoing process.

Continuous recruitment means establishing systems at your center that will help you fill vacancies as they occur by quickly generating a pool of applicants for consideration. Continuous recruitment is important in the early care and education profession because of the impact turnover has on children, families, and teachers. Continuous recruitment is a series of operational tasks that are addressed daily, weekly, and monthly, not a single set of activities that commence when a teacher gives notice and resigns. It forms the foundation of program stability by enabling you to quickly respond when a job vacancy does occur.

Like most organizational issues, there is no simple recipe for implementing a continuous recruitment plan at your center. Continuous recruitment is a little bit like curriculum: it needs to be individualized. It should reflect the unique needs and characteristics of your program and the available resources for recruitment. This chapter presents a variety of techniques and strategies that will help you develop a continuous recruitment plan for your program. The process begins with thinking about your current staffing patterns.

A foolish act done over and over again will not improve things.

West African proverb

Being Prepared

In the early care and education field, being prepared for turnover should be part of every center administrator's mindset. An undergirding principle of survival is to anticipate staffing challenges and have a plan to cope with the interim period between a teacher's resignation and her replacement with an adequately trained and oriented new hire.

There are a variety of staffing models that rely on substitutes, floaters, and teaching teams to lessen the impact of a teacher change on children, families, co-workers, and program administrators. Using teaching teams and having additional floating staff who can fill in when a teacher leaves are two strategies for coping that are widely used in the field.

Use teaching teams. Many centers rely on teaching teams rather than the more traditional staffing of a teacher and assistant teacher in a classroom. When teams are in place and working well, programs are less likely to experience the negative effects of turnover. Teams can comprise three or more teachers who work together planning curricula and managing several classrooms. When one team member leaves, children and parents have a shared history with the remaining members of the teaching team and experience some stability from their continued presence.

Unfortunately, the time it takes to recruit and train a replacement teacher puts additional stress and work responsibilities on the team members remaining. Part of being prepared for turnover is having a plan to provide support to the team members responsible for the ongoing stability of the classrooms.

Use floating staff. Many programs use additional staff (either substitutes or floaters) to replace teachers who are absent due to vacation, sick leave, or medical and maternity leave. Typically, floating staff and substitutes have completed some professional preparation for the teaching role, like orientation and pre-service training. In addition, they have had experienced in the classroom, often under the guidance of a more experience and tenured teacher, which results in knowledge about children, curriculum, center culture, and so on.

Programs using substitutes and floating staff are often the best prepared to temporarily replace a departing teacher without as much disruption to children, families, and teachers. Floaters and experienced substitutes can help hold things together as the recruitment process unfolds. If your program is not using teams, floating staff, or substitutes, consider these strategies as part of your plan to address turnover.

Networking

In the case of recruitment, who you know is an important variable. Contacts within the local business and early childhood professional community, knowing who else is advertising for teachers, and having abundant sources and leads for finding good applicants are crucial. Develop your own list of networking contacts using the form in Appendix A. Here are some possibilities.

Join local groups of business professionals. Because directors are responsible for such a wide range of tasks, it is easy to become isolated from other professionals and programs. Isolation, though, makes recruitment even more challenging. Make a conscious effort to broaden your professional contacts in your business community. Join the local Rotary Club or Chamber of Commerce. Share information about your program. These contacts may yield surprising connections when a job vacancy does occur.

Join a directors' support group. Many directors view their participation in their local director's network as their lifeline to sanity. Only other directors really understand the issues you face administering an early childhood program. If there isn't a directors' support group in your community, connect with a few other directors and start one so you can share information and resources and find emotional support for your successes and challenges, including those related to recruitment.

Other directors need not be viewed as competitors. Networking among programs can create opportunities for administrators and their teachers to visit each other's programs, share their ideas and interests, and support one another in carrying out their complex jobs. Explore the programs in your vicinity and meet the directors to see if you have common interests, common needs, and common challenges on which to build collaborative relationships.

Join state and national professional associations. Attending professional meetings and workshops is a way to be visible and active in the professional community, a networking idea sure to help you and your program in many ways, including with recruitment. Administrators who present workshops at professional conferences are not only building their leadership skills, but also becoming savvy recruiters. They know that participants at their workshop may some day be job candidates at their door. Here are four well-known national associations in the early care and education field that you will want to contact.

- The National Association for the Education of Young Children (NAEYC) is a membership and advocacy organization with local and state affiliates throughout the country. NAEYC publishes *Young Children*, a bimonthly journal for professionals, and accredits early childhood programs through the NAEYC Academy for Early Childhood Program Accreditation. Contact NAEYC at www.naeyc.org.

- The National Child Care Association (NCCA) is a professional trade association focusing on the needs of licensed, private care, and education programs. NCCA provides a Child Care Professional Credential (CCPC) for teachers and the National Administrator Credential (NAC), a management credential for directors. Contact NCCA at www.ncca.org.

- The Association for Childhood Education International (ACEI) publishes *Childhood Education*, a bimonthly journal covering research, practice, and public policy. ACEI is also a membership and advocacy group that promotes sound educational practice from infancy to adolescence. Contact ACEI at www.acei.org.

- The National Association of Child Care Professionals (NACCP), a trade membership organization, publishes a newsletter, *Professional Connections*, and hosts an annual conference. NACCP also administers an accreditation system for early childhood programs. Contact NACCP at www.naccp.org.

Some of these organizations have job boards and provide resources and recruitment services for their members. There are many other professional organizations and associations that may have affiliate groups in your area. Learn more about them and add them to your networking list. Members of these groups are potential contacts for generating applicants when the need arises.

Connect with faculty at local colleges. An emphasis on formal academic preparation for early childhood practitioners has increased the number of colleges and universities that train teachers. Many community colleges offer one- and two-year certificates in early care and education as well as Child Development Associate (CDA) training. Colleges and universities offer baccalaureate degrees in early care and education, child development, or early childhood education. All serve as excellent sources for recruiting new graduates as well as a source for part-time employees. Making personal contacts with faculty teaching at these institutions could help bring interested and qualified applicants to your door.

Many college programs value opportunities for their students to get field experiences in high-quality programs in the community. Find out about credential and degree programs offered in your area, and get involved. Offer unpaid and paid internships to students enrolled in college degree programs. Create connections with local colleges for placement of Federal Work Study students. Such opportunities give students meaningful, applied experiences and in the process allow you to match students' personalities, interests, and skills with your program staffing needs. Students in need of short-term employment between semesters and during the summer may turn out to be candidates for future positions at your center.

In addition, volunteer your center as an observation site and welcome student observers. Offer to speak to senior level classes. By sharing your expertise, experiences, stories, and program culture with students, you plant a seed of interest in your center as a place to consider for employment after graduation.

Contact local resource and referral agencies. Within most communities, there are a variety of training and resource and referral organizations that are supported by local, state, and federal funds or through private funding from foundations and individuals. These organizations are typically connected to the early care and education profession in many ways and provide a cadre of resources and services. Find out about such organizations in your area and access any services for which you may be eligible. Many of them will lend support in your recruitment efforts.

Contact other community organizations. If you think about recruitment as a long-term strategy, it makes sense to contact local high schools, park and recreation centers, or other community-based groups where teenagers and young adults hang out. Volunteer to present a workshop on careers in early childhood education at your local high school career fair. Propose your center as a place where a babysitter's certification course can be offered. Work with local groups that organize teens for community service projects and get them involved in your program. These long-term recruitment strategies can pay rich dividends in the years ahead.

Advertising

Two types of advertising are typically used in early care and education programs. The first is enrollment advertising to recruit clients or families to use your services and fill your program. The second is recruitment advertising aimed at staffing your program. All of the advertising you do is important and gets your program's name out in your community, makes others aware of the services you offer, and gives information about how you implement your program. In continuous recruitment, the focus is on recruitment advertising.

Recruitment advertising takes many forms—some are expensive and some free or inexpensive. The key in continuous recruitment is to take advantage of as many free or inexpensive strategies as you can on a regular basis and identify where and when to judiciously spend resources on paid advertising.

Free or inexpensive advertising. Posting job announcements on job boards at area colleges and universities, businesses like retail or specialty stores, and religious institutions gets the information about your job opportunities out to new audiences. Ask parents and staff to take job announcements with them to their churches, mosques, or synagogues as well as to leisure activities where potential job seekers might take exercise or enrichment classes or attend professional networking meetings. Post announcements in clear view at events that might attract potential applicants, like parenting or sibling classes. Be creative. Brainstorm new places to get the word out.

Plan to replace and replenish your job postings regularly. Community bulletin boards are cleared on a regular basis and will need new announcements. You will want the notices to look attractive and professional. To keep them that way, you will need to check on your postings and replace worn, torn, or dog-eared ones.

Paid advertising. Paid advertising is available from many sources. Community newspapers, the Internet, job banks, and professional publications all sell advertising space. The challenge is to find a good match between your financial resources and the strategy that generates the most applicants for you to consider.

Paid advertising in daily or weekly newspapers is often an expensive proposition. Listing the announcement so it doesn't get lost is an additional challenge. Choose a classification that will get attention. For example, if teaching positions are listed alphabetically in a category called professional, make sure to place your ad where the most potential applicants will see it. If the ad begins with "early care and education teacher," will potential applicants think to look alphabetically under "e" or should you change the title to "teacher - early childhood" to attract more readers? Investigate your options to maximize your exposure.

Increasingly, print media are taking advantage of electronic media. Job advertisements published in a newspaper may also appear on the paper's Website. Don't forget to ask if such options are available to you.

Components of an ad. Effective ads have similar components. Typically, they include:

- Job title and brief description of the position
- Qualifications, both required and preferred
- Status—full-time or part-time
- Schedule—work hours and days
- Location, particularly in large cities with long commutes
- Program features that might be important to applicants, like accreditation status or teaching philosophy
- Contact information—where to send resumes, how applications will be accepted (fax, e-mail, etc.)
- When and how to apply (times to call, in person, submit resume)
- Nondiscrimination policy statement—that the center is an equal opportunity employer

Remember, in writing your ad don't explicitly or implicitly express a preference for candidates based on a protected status (e.g., sex, age, race, national origin).

Not all ads are created equal. Here are some hints from experts about how to get the most from your ad. Although helpful, these ideas may be costly. Consider a variety of strategies, and then pick the ones that you think will garner the most attention for the money.

- Bigger is better. The eye is drawn to larger ads, particularly if they are well designed.

- Don't scrimp on design. The visual appeal of your advertisement may determine whether it gets read or not.

- Add design features like logos, screening, or highlighted text. Include visuals that make your school unique, like buildings, photographs of children, or images of teachers at work.

- Use a catchy opening.

- Say what you have to say differently from everyone else.

- Describe the job sufficiently; however, leave readers wanting to know more. Remember, the purpose of any job ad is to draw potential applicants. If your ad leads readers to call you rather than another advertiser, you will have more applicants to consider.

- Avoid using abbreviations and jargon. You may know what they mean, but readers may not. Some abbreviations are regional or local, others may just be unknown. Avoid misunderstanding by eliminating jargon completely.

- Personalize your ad—make it unique.

Check out employment ads from the various sources—newspapers, professional journals, newsletters, job placement boards, and other sources. Start a collection of attractive ads so you can incorporate their features into your advertisements. Include your last few ads as well, so you can compare them with ads others are using.

Early Childhood Educators

We are looking for Childcare Professionals to work with our most precious resource...our employees' children.

Our on-site child development center in our **Lisle, IL** office provides a Montessori environment that nurtures our children, while stimulating their creativity and expanding their horizons. We offer a bright, energetic workplace to our employees, and strive to provide the same dynamic surroundings for our children.

Our state-of-the-art development center provides exceptionally equipped indoor and outdoor space for youngsters to grow and learn. Successful candidates should have a BS degree in education or a related field, a desire for AMI Montessori certification, and 1-3 years experience working with young children and infants. A Nursing background is desirable for our Assistants in our Infant environments.

We have Child Development Centers located in our offices around the world; Long Island, NY; Chicago, IL; Boston, MA; Herndon, VA; London, England and Sydney, Australia.

Computer Associates International, Inc., *(NYSE:CA),* the world leader in mission-critical business computing, has more than 17,500 employees and had revenue of $5.3 billion in fiscal year 1999. We provide software, support, and integration services in more than 100 countries around the world.

We offer a generous compensation package with a long list of benefits that nobody else can match, including 401(k) and profit sharing plans, company-paid medical and dental coverage, onsite fitness center, tuition reimbursement and tremendous growth opportunity. Complimentary continental breakfast served daily. Send your resume today.

Computer Associates International, Inc.
Attention: BB
One Computer Associates Plaza
Islandia, NY 11749

Tel: 1-800-454-3788 • Fax: 1-800-962-9224
Visit our Web site at: www.cai.com

© 1999 Computer Associates International, Inc., Islandia, NY 11749. Compute[...]
grams, regardless of race, color, creed, religion, sex, sexual orientation, age, dis[...]

Software superior by design.

Where to place ads. Crafting an eye-catching ad is only part of the equation in optimizing advertising to ensure successful recruitment outcomes. Deciding on the right venue for maximal exposure is the other part. Here are your options.

- **Newspapers.** Newspapers publish job advertisements as a regular feature. Consider carefully in which paper to publish your job ad. Readership is the key issue. Check with circulation departments to obtain readership information. Readership varies weekly, monthly, and seasonally. Place your ads for Sunday through Thursday readership. Friday and Saturday usually have lower readership. Analyze the numbers carefully and be sure the demographics of the publication's readership matches your needs.

  Consider suburban or community newspapers and free job placement newspapers. Community newspapers are delivered on a different schedule from daily newspapers and, because of the local flavor, may result in a different readership. Free job magazines may have wide distribution in grocery and retail stores but may not target the population that you want to reach.

- **Professional periodicals.** Local and state affiliates of professional associations often have newsletters that accept job advertisements for a fraction of the cost of paid advertising in the print media. Find out if teachers are avid readers of any other publications in your area and consider placing job advertisements in those publications. Also, consider related fields for which professional preparation may parallel that of the early childhood field like psychology, elementary education, recreation, speech and language therapy, social work, or nursing.

- **Student newspapers.** College student newspapers and student-sponsored campus publications are another possibility for paid advertising. Usually less expensive than other print media advertising, these publications reach students who may be nearing the end of their degree programs or may be interested in part-time or internship experiences.

- **Job place bureaus.** Colleges and universities have job placement bureaus that post available job ads for alumni of the university to access in their job searches. Fees are typically affordable and job opportunities are usually posted for longer periods of time. Explore these services, focusing especially on those universities that have trained the successful teachers on your staff. If you have more than one graduate from the same university on your staff, it is probably worthwhile to investigate ways to get your job announcements out to current alumni of that institution as well as to students who are nearing graduation. In addition to college job-placement bureaus, there are many private job placement services whose mission is to recruit candidates for different businesses. Explore these options carefully as fees vary widely.

Thinking Outside the Box

The heart of developing a continuous recruitment plan for your center is thinking of how recruitment can be tied to virtually all other systems and activities of your program. When you conceptualize recruitment in broad terms like this, it is amazing what creative strategies you'll come up with to attract high-quality candidates to your center as a place of employment. Here are a few that some directors have tried.

Parent referral programs. Notifying parents of recruitment needs is an interesting recruitment strategy. When parents are empowered to make referrals from their personal child care networks, it makes them part of the recruitment team. Parents may identify potential employees from babysitting pools, friends, neighborhoods, or their workplace.

Some programs enhance their partnership with parents by providing incentives to parents who refer applicants. Incentives take many forms, including discounts on services, finder's fees, recognition in the center's newsletter, handwritten thank you notes, and invitations to serve on interview and selection committees.

Staff referral programs. You can use a similar referral program with staff. When you help teachers join the continuous recruitment process, you are strengthening the partnership between teachers and administration. Recognizing that everyone is part of the recruitment team is important—a concept worth introducing, developing, and nurturing in your program. In schools with the established norm that staff are valued partners in attracting new colleagues, there is often an ancillary benefit of increased staff commitment to the center's goals.

Enlisting teachers in the recruitment team can be done formally or informally. When enlistment is formal, teachers may need training on what to do, what to say, and how to go about talking to their colleagues in ethical and responsible ways. Formal training helps staff see recruitment as a worthwhile activity. Business cards and written material about the program help teachers share at professional meetings, training events, workshops, and conferences. When approaching it informally, administrators can simply suggest that teachers let them know if they know of adults who have the required credentials.

Programs enhance shared recruitment efforts by providing incentives to teachers who refer applicants. Incentives may include finder's fees, recognition in the staff newsletter, handwritten thank you notes, invitations to serve on interview and selection teams, and opportunities to mentor newly hired teachers.

Job fairs and career days. Participate in job fairs and career days held in your area. Visibility at events like these can lead adults who have not considered early childhood education as a career option.

Internet. One of the newest sources of applicants is the Internet. Consider developing a Website for your center. This will help ensure there is a visible, easy link to current and future job possibilities. Find out from frequent Internet surfers (perhaps among your parents or staff) which job-search sites are the most popular and explore ways to link your Web page to them.

Collaborative recruiting efforts. Increasingly, early care and education programs are joining together to recruit. Several programs may advertise jointly, lowering the overall cost of advertising and generating applicants for all involved programs to consider. That is what program administrators in Evanston, Illinois did. They pooled their resources for advertising and created a larger ad than any one of them could have afforded alone—a win-win solution to the problem of high advertising costs.

Other collaborations have used professional recruiters to broaden the search. Professional recruiters often have a national focus and conduct many of the recruitment activities that are beyond the scope of an individual director, like visiting colleges and universities with early childhood/child development programs around the country. They also cast a wider net—looking in nontraditional places for potential applicants.

Getting Started

Take a few minutes now to jot down some notes about how you will begin implementing a continuous recruitment plan at your center. Complete Exercise 3, noting changes you might make in staffing patterns to be more prepared when a vacancy occurs, networking contacts you plan to initiate, advertising strategies you can put in place, and any other innovative and outside-the-box ideas that might help you achieve your goal of having a seamless, continuous system for recruiting high-quality teachers.

Implementing a Continuous Recruitment Plan

✔ Staffing changes I'll make to be better prepared ...

_____

_____

_____

_____

✔ Networking strategies I plan to use ...

_____

_____

_____

_____

✔ Advertising strategies I plan to use ...

_____

_____

_____

_____

✔ Other recruitment strategies I plan to use ...

_____

_____

_____

_____

An Unexpected Benefit

Programs that implement a plan of continuous recruitment experience an unexpected benefit. Public relations between the school, the neighborhood, the educational community, and the larger community are enhanced. The reputation of the program improves as you expand involvement in professional networking. All these strategies position you for recognition as a specialist in early care and education in your community. When the community's image of your program broadens to include it as a great place to work, you will be more likely to be successful in your recruitment efforts. In the process, you will probably also bolster your center's enrollment.

CHAPTER 3

Maximizing the "Fit"

Perhaps the greatest predictor of success in finding the perfect candidate for a teaching vacancy in your center is a clear understanding of what <u>fit</u> means to you, your staff, and your program. This chapter will help you identify criteria for selecting the candidate who most closely matches the job requirements as well as your program's culture, needs, and expectations—the candidate who is the best fit. Fit criteria spell out the special characteristics, expectations, knowledge, skills, philosophy, instructional approaches, and all the other qualities that make the job and your program unique.

Thinking about the recruitment process in terms of goodness of fit requires a subtle but important shift in thinking—a shift from hiring to selecting. If you think of your role as *hiring* the most qualified candidate, the tendency is to focus on the paper qualifications of applicants, looking for that one resume that stands out from all the rest. If, on the other hand, you think of your role as *selecting* the right candidate, the most qualified person on paper may or may not be the right person for the position. Selecting implies a careful analysis of fit.

In this chapter we'll look at two kinds of fit—the fit between the individual and the job you are seeking to fill and the fit between the individual and the total program. For every recruitment scenario, the issues and fit criteria will be slightly different. That's because every individual, job, and center is unique.

Individuals Are Unique

No doubt about it, the complexity of human variation defies simple descriptions. The candidates that walk through the front door of your center will represent the full range of personality typologies. They will look, act, and think differently from one another. The key for effective hiring decisions is appreciating what specific personal and professional characteristics are best suited to the position you are seeking to fill and the context of that position, your center's culture.

Some of the Ways Individuals Differ

- Knowledge of child development, effective instructional practices, classroom management practices, and different curricula

- Skill—ability to carry out knowledge (for example, maintain classroom order, assess children's growth and development, lead a circle time)

- Dispositions and temperament (for example, tendency to be nurturing, playful, curious, optimistic, flexible, resilient, risk-taking, or self-starting)

- Teaching style—how knowledge, skills, and dispositions come together

- Work-style preferences (for example, likes to work alone or as part of a team)

- Physical limitations and energy level

- Needs and expectations for autonomy, structure, variety, neatness, control, intellectual challenge, or level of compensation

- Interests and talents in areas such as music, art, drama, literature, athletics

- Values and beliefs about different educational practices such as appropriate goals for children, the role of the teacher, the importance of diversity, the role of parents, and the importance of inclusion

- Learning style and sensory modality preference (visual, auditory, or kinesthetic)

- Educational philosophy (for example, Montessori or Waldorf)

- Outside commitments and obligations (for example, works at a soup kitchen on weekends, cares for an elderly parent, or sings in the church choir)

- Personal ethics and integrity

- Professional orientation (perceptions about work as "just a job" or a career, degree of involvement in career advancement opportunities)

People differ in their needs, expectations, values, degree of flexibility, and a host of other small and big ways. This diversity is what gives richness to your program, but it is also, no doubt, what gives you grey hairs as an administrator. Good selection systems are based on the premise that diversity is a desirable characteristic of programs, but too much diversity can result in turmoil. Your role in the interviewing and selection process is to determine how the individual's needs, expectations, special talents, and skills both match the demands of the job and support your vision to have a diverse but unified staff in vision and practice.

Amanda was a center director for about four years before she participated in management training that stresses the importance of recognizing and appreciating individual differences. Prior to undergoing the training, she made several hiring decisions that resulted in poor management outcomes. Either the newly hired teacher remained on the job for only a short time or stayed but failed to live up to expectations of professional practice. Learning about different styles of thinking and learning—the multiple ways that people perceive information and make decisions based on these perceptions—had a direct impact on her subsequent hiring decisions. Amanda states, "The biggest mistake I made in the past was hiring staff just like myself. Of course I was more comfortable hiring staff with a similar personality type, just like wearing old shoes is more comfortable than wearing new ones that give you needed support." Amanda has come to realize that to develop a well-balanced team she needs staff who are down-to-earth and operate from experience, as well as staff who are future oriented and look for the meaning and purpose of things. Her team needs well-organized staff, preferring order and routine, as well as spontaneous, flexible staff capable of adaptive behavior.

If we were all alike, we'd only need one of us

Lilian Katz

Some of the ways that individuals differ will be readily apparent on their resumes; others you will need to determine in your face-to-face interview. Still others can only be assessed from speaking with former employers and colleagues or watching the person in action. Of course, there are some characteristics that are more important to determine up front than others. What is the candidate's previous experience working with young children? What stage is the person in his or her career? What does the candidate need in the way of intellectual challenge, variety, autonomy, creativity, and opportunities for advancement? If you look at individuals through a goodness-of-fit lens, the best person for the job may not necessarily be the most qualified on paper. The right fit might mean hiring a person who can stretch and grow in a position; one who will make a long-term commitment to your center if the working conditions and organizational climate support continued personal and professional growth.

In addition to the typical selection criteria such as level of education, specialized training, and experience, maximizing the fit means looking at work-relevant personality characteristics that are more subtle and subjective but critical in ensuring a candidate's success in your program. One way to think about work-relevant personality characteristics is to think about the attributes of a good teacher. Read the items in the following table. These are probably some of the attributes you will use when you develop fit criteria for a specific job vacancy at your center.

Now take a few minutes to complete Exercise 4 found on page 28. Think in general terms about the characteristics of a good employee. There may be some conceptual overlap between the items you come up with and those you on the previous list. However, keeping them separate is a helpful reminder that the most successful teachers you've hired are capable and competent in their professional practice as well as successful members of your organization.

Characteristics of a Good Teacher

Characteristics	Examples of abilities, attitudes, behaviors, dispositions, and skills
Articulate	Communicates so children understand
Available	Willing to devote time; available to children and their parents
Caring	Understanding, kind, compassionate, empathic, friendly, warm
Challenging	Challenges children to think; sets high expectations
Committed	Dedicated and devoted to teaching
Congenial	Gets along with co-workers and parents
Creative	Uses a variety of teaching strategies
Dynamic	Lively, energetic, enthusiastic
Fair	Does not have favorites
Flexible	Able to depart from fixed schedule and deal with the unexpected
Fun	Has a good sense of humor
Individualizes	Meets the needs of individual children including those with learning challenges or from a variety of backgrounds and cultures
Intelligent	Bright and capable
Knowledgeable	Familiar with different instructional methods and materials as well as children's concerns, needs, and developmental levels
Motivating	Promotes active involvement in learning; makes learning fun
Open	Open-minded; sees things from other perspectives
Organized	Able to organize space, materials, time, and lesson plans
Patient	Even-tempered
Pleasant	Smiles often; uses effective voice tone and gestures
Prepared	Prepares well before teaching
Professional	Conscientious about carrying out responsibilities; does not let personal problems interfere with teaching
Reflective	Reflects upon his/her performance as a teacher; accepts criticism
Respected	Keeps order in the classroom; is in control

Adapted from Weinstein, C. (1989). Teacher education students' preconceptions of teaching. Journal of Teacher Education, 40(2), 53-60.

Characteristics of a Good Employee

Characteristics	Examples of abilities, attitudes, behaviors, dispositions, and skills

No doubt your work-relevant characteristics for a good employee include such things as being punctual, conscientious, and honest; taking initiative; supporting others; and following through with commitments to co-workers and supervisors. Some of these characteristics may seem mundane, but collectively they are critical to smooth working relations in a program. Because work-related personality characteristics are more difficult to identify and evaluate during the interviewing process, you will want to think of ways to assess the traits you consider are crucial for an applicant's fit with your program. We'll explore some of these fit criteria later.

There are many assessments available to assist you in your quest to determine the fit between an individual and job available at your center. Appendix B is a tool you may find useful in gathering data about a candidate's professional orientation. Appendix C is an assessment tool designed to gather data about a prospective candidate's beliefs and values. There are no right or wrong answers in completing this instrument. It is designed to determine the degree of fit between a candidate and your program's collective values and beliefs.

Jobs Are Unique

Like individuals, each job is also unique. Some of the ways early childhood teaching jobs differ are obvious—ages of the children served, level of expertise required, work schedule, and the level of pay and benefits received. But jobs also differ in many less obvious but equally important ways—degree of autonomy and decision-making responsibility, number and type of meetings required, expectations for ongoing professional development, and expectations for parent involvement. Read the following list, add additional ways jobs differ at your center.

In many ways each job at a center is an extension of that center's culture, philosophy, and collective goals for children and families. The uniqueness comes from the specific requirements of the position as they relate to the age of the children, group size, classroom space and resources, and co-worker expectations.

Job descriptions—your fit criteria. Job descriptions are a tool to provide guidance to applicants about the job's specific duties. Well-written job descriptions tell the applicant what is expected and how to perform the job satisfactorily. Job descriptions usually include job requirements (like education and experience), job responsibilities and major tasks (including descriptions of what the job holder does and tasks for which he or she is held accountable), special skills and abilities needed to do the job (particularly those unique to the position), to whom the employee reports in the organization, and sometimes the salary range.

You will want to make sure the job description for the position for which you are recruiting is up to date and complete. If you don't have good job descriptions on file, involve teachers in helping you identify the job requirements and responsibilities, and the skills and abilities necessary for a position, ensuring that the job descriptions you have reflect your own and your teachers' current expectations for the job.

Some of the Ways Jobs Differ

- General knowledge, specialized knowledge, and specific skills required for the age level and special needs of children being served

- Degree of responsibility required for planning and implementing the curriculum

- Level of pay and type of benefits

- Job schedule (regular work hours, planning time, and meeting time)

- Expectations for parent involvement

- Degree of autonomy for making decisions

- Degree of routine or variety

- Degree of intellectual challenge

- Physical demands for lifting, holding, bending, walking, and/or running

- Degree of supervision provided by supervisor and degree of supervision exercised over others (assistant teachers, aides, volunteers)

- Physical environment (for example, room size, lighting, equipment, and instructional supplies)

- Expectations for co-worker relations (for example, team teaching, joint unit planning)

- Number of meetings and amount of paperwork and record keeping required

- Expectations for ongoing professional development

When a job description is accurately and appropriately drafted, it can serve not only as a guide for applications, it can also inform the reasonable accommodation process for disabled candidates and staff members and provide a foundation for staff performance evaluations. But remember, government agencies and courts regard job descriptions as prime evidence of job requirements. Be certain to consult an employment attorney, legal aid organization, or human resources consultant to review your center's job descriptions. Make it your center's practice to review and update all job descriptions annually.

The job requirements detailed in the job description should be comprehensive enough to give a clear picture of the necessary qualifications and/or their equivalents. This of course includes professional preparation and experience. Many programs have adopted language from the National Association for the Education of Young Children (NAEYC) as criteria for different positions. For example, NAEYC recommends that early childhood teacher assistants (staff who implement program activities under direct supervision) be high school graduates or the equivalent, be trained in early childhood education or child development, and participate in ongoing professional development. NAEYC recommends that teachers (staff who are responsible for the care and education of a group of children from birth through five) have a minimum of a Child Development Associate Credential (CDA) or associate's degree in early childhood or child development and preferably a baccalaureate degree with specialized training in early childhood education.

The second part of a good job description details job responsibilities and major tasks. This section of the job description clarifies *what* applicants will be doing and describes the tasks for which they will be responsible. Some job responsibilities and major tasks will emerge as you and your teachers consider the unique cultural and philosophical characteristics of your school. Others will emerge from thinking about the functions of the job—the things that must happen to make the classroom work. Be comprehensive but concise. Include the responsibilities that you and your staff are able to identify that present a clear picture of what applicants must do to be effective.

Although job responsibilities and major tasks are important, you obviously won't be able to list everything that a teacher has to do. As you refine your job description, select those tasks essential to ensuring high performance. Then add a general statement about "other duties as required," to remind applicants that the responsibilities listed are not all-inclusive. This helps prevent misunderstanding later on about expectations.

One way to approach the writing of a job description is to think about what *competence* means in relation to a specific job. What general and specific knowledge does the applicant need to have? What skills are necessary to perform the job satisfactorily? What dispositions are essential or desirable to be successful in the position? Summarize these items in the last section of the job description.

Job descriptions are essentially fit criteria. They allow programs to consider how well an applicant's professional preparation, experience, skills, abilities, and dispositions match what the job requires. The following is an example of a job description that can serve as a template for your work.

Head Teacher

The head teacher is responsible for the supervision and management of a classroom in accord with the goals and curriculum plan of the Hickory Woods Child Development Center. The principal duties of the head teacher include: develop action plans, carry out activities on a daily basis, evaluate the effectiveness of child development activities, supervise staff assigned to assist in the classroom, ensure the safety and physical well-being of the children, maintain regular communication with parents, and contribute to the effective operation of the center's overall program.

Accountability: The head teacher reports to the child care center director.

Responsibilities

- Plan and conduct an effective child development program to meet the physical, social, emotional, and intellectual needs of each child. This should be done based on the goals and general curriculum plan of the Hickory Woods Child Development Center.

- Ensure that routines are carried out in a manner that is prompt, hygienic, and consistent with good child development principles. This includes routines related to diapering, toilet training, hand washing, tooth brushing, eating, napping, and transitioning between activities.

- Ensure the children's safety through constant supervision, effective arrangement of space, proper maintenance of equipment, and regular practice of fire drills and other emergency procedures.

- Operate the classroom in compliance with all licensing standards, paying particular attention to ensure that standards prohibiting corporal punishment are obeyed.

- Provide supervision to all staff assigned to the classroom and include staff in planning assignments.

- Create a pleasant, inviting classroom atmosphere in which children feel comfortable and secure.

- Provide positive guidance to help children develop self-control.

- Provide experiences that promote individual self-expression in conversation, imaginative play, and creativity.

- Provide a variety of language stimulation activities.

- Provide experience involving thinking skills such as generalizing, classifying, sorting, and problem solving.

- Provide a variety of opportunities to help children develop and sustain appropriate relationships with others.

- Ensure that parents receive adequate information about their children's experiences at the center through daily contact and regularly scheduled parent conferences.

- Maintain written records designed to evaluate each child as well as the class as a whole.

- Contribute to the operation of the center by participating in staff meetings and sharing information gained through attendance at workshops and professional reading.

- Work as a member of a team to ensure continuity of curriculum and a high standard of quality in all classrooms in the center.

- Perform other duties as required.

Job Requirements

Education and Experience

- A college degree in child development or early childhood education and at least one year of experience teaching in a part-day or full-day program for preschool children; or

- A college degree in an appropriate human service or education field (e.g., psychology, special education, music, social work), including some courses in child development, and at least two years teaching experience in a part-day or full-day program for preschool children.

Personal Qualities

Must be physically able to perform the job of a teacher of young children. Must have a warm, supportive attitude toward children. Must be reliable. Must be flexible in receiving assignments or adapting to changes in the program. Must be willing to accept supervision in order to improve work performance.

Adapted from Perreault, J., & Neugebauer, R. (1998). Developing your employee handbook: Job descriptions. In B. Neugebauer & R. Neugebauer (Eds.), The art of leadership: Managing early childhood organizations (pp. 174-77). Redmond, WA: Exchange Press. Reprinted with permission.

A key consideration—salaries and benefits. When you interview an applicant, you'll want to be sure there is a good fit between the salary and benefits you can offer and what the applicant needs and expects to receive. Most directors have had the experience of hiring a strong candidate for a teaching position only to find out three or six months later that the teacher is unable continue in the job because the salary or benefits are inadequate. Sometimes in our desperation to fill a position or our zeal to "sell" our program to a strong candidate, we downplay salary and benefits as a critical determinant of job satisfaction and long-term commitment to the program. Not covering this issue openly and candidly during the interviewing and screening process can cause problems down the road.

Reaching the end of a job interview, the director asks a young teacher fresh out of college, "What starting salary were you thinking about?"

The applicant replies confidently, "In the neighborhood of $40,000."

The director says, "Well, what would you say to a package of four weeks paid vacation, 14 paid holidays, two round-trip tickets and registration for any national conference you'd like to attend, full medical and dental insurance coverage, a matching retirement fund to 50% of your salary, free child care for your daughter, and a Volkswagen Jetta?"

The applicant sits straight up and says, "Wow! Are you kidding?"

The director replies, "Yeah, but you started it!"

Source unknown

In the discussion earlier about infrastructure issues that challenge early care and education, compensation emerged as a central weakness of the field—not just an issue for individual programs. The goal of identifying fit criteria related to salary and benefits is to make sure that your center's compensation package is clearly understood so that the applicant who accepts a job offer does not become disillusioned after he or she begins. This is especially important for young adults entering the workforce and accepting their first full-time teaching position. Many new teachers have idealized notions of what it is like to be an early childhood educator. Open and clear communication during the recruitment process about the nature of the position, the starting salary and benefits package, and the potential for increases can help shape more realistic expectations.

Because low salaries and benefits are a professionwide infrastructure issue, you may be able to differentiate your program in the marketplace if you carefully assess your total salary and benefits package. The development of a career ladder and salary scale for your center is one way to achieve this. Salary scales are designed to support clarity and fairness in employment practices. They should measure the monetary value of employees' contributions on different job factors—level of responsibility, training, experience, and performance, and then weight each factor with programmatic expectations. Your salary schedule thus reflects the resource allocation priorities identified by your program. It also clearly defines the path for advancement to higher compensation.

Take a close look at the salary ranges for the different positions in your program to ensure they reflect both vertical and horizontal equity. In other words, jobs with comparable requirements and levels of responsibility should have comparable salary ranges (horizontal equity). Jobs with increasing levels of responsibility should receive commensurately greater compensation (vertical equity). It is beyond the scope of this book to cover the specific steps for constructing a salary scale and career ladder, but the reference list at the end of this book includes several resources to help you get started.

Less than half of early childhood programs offer benefits that most workers in the workforce consider standard—paid health insurance, vacation leave, sick leave, tuition reimbursement. However, in the benefits category directors have some discretion to craft a package for a desired candidate. Many programs with limited financial resources are able to create different but equitable benefits packages for their employees by offering a menu of options. Look at the range of personal and profession benefits in Exercise 5 as you think about ways to offer a combination of possibilities to a potential new employee.

Personal benefits

- ❏ Disability insurance
- ❏ Health insurance
  (____% paid by employer)
- ❏ Family health insurance
  (___% paid by employer)
- ❏ Vacation (____ number of days)
- ❏ Personal leave (____ number of days)
- ❏ Sick leave (____ number of days)
- ❏ Life insurance
  (____% paid by employer)
- ❏ Retirement plan
  (____% paid by employer)
- ❏ Dental insurance
  (____% paid by employer)
- ❏ Vision insurance
  (____% paid by employer)
- ❏ Accidental injury/catastrophic illness
- ❏ Maternity leave
  (____% paid by employer)
- ❏ Jury duty
  (____% paid by employer)
- ❏ Child care
  (____% paid by employer)
- ❏ Other _____

Professional benefits

- ❏ Membership in a professional association
- ❏ Released time to visit other centers
- ❏ Tuition reimbursement for college classes
- ❏ Subscription to professional journals
- ❏ Conference or workshop registration fees
- ❏ Credential or certification fees
- ❏ Other _____

"It's the board's idea of a comprehensive medical benefits package."

In addition to the benefits noted in Exercise 5, there are other specialized benefits you may be able to offer that are unique to your program. You may be in a position, for example, to offer a flexible work schedule, to structure a job-sharing arrangement, to provide CDA training, or to mentor an employee in a specific curriculum. When you focus on maximizing the fit between the individual and the job, including these intangible benefits, all kinds of creative possibilities may surface.

How and what an administrator can offer in terms of benefits will differ from program to program. So too will the employee and employer contributions to each benefit. It is essential, however, that candidates be able to decipher exactly what is included in your benefits package. You need to be absolutely clear about what you offer, what you as an employer pay, what the employee contribution if any will be, when employees are eligible for each benefit, and the total cost of the benefits package to the employee. Equity and legal considerations must guide your decision making in this area.

Centers Are Unique

Every center has its own culture—a composite of its history, traditions, philosophy, leadership, norms in the way things are done, collective values, and much, much more. Maximizing the fit means taking into consideration how the individual candidate will *fit into* and *add* to the rich diversity already present in the center. Here are just some of the ways that centers differ.

Some of the Ways Centers Differ

- Educational philosophy as it relates to appropriate curriculum, the role of teachers, and expectations for children

- History and traditions

- Shared values and beliefs; organizational ethics

- Norms about everyday demeanor and how things should be done (for example, degree of formality in how children address teachers, expectations for noise level, appropriate dress for staff)

- Legal governing structure, size, and program options for children and families

- Division of labor, workload expectations, accountability systems, and opportunities for advancement

- Leadership and management practices including decision-making and problem-solving processes, goal setting, supervision, performance appraisal practices, and emphasis on equity and fairness

- Parent relations—frequency of, type of involvement in, and expectations about parents' role in program operations and governance

- Instructional practices, including daily routines and child assessment procedures

- Co-worker relations and expectations for collaboration

- Communication processes, including formal and informal patterns of verbal and written communication and approaches to conflict resolution

- Physical environment—the arrangement of space and the availability of instructional resources

- Collective expertise, talents, and skills of the staff

- Innovativeness and technology—the extent to which the center adapts to change and encourages staff to find creative ways to solve problems

- Accounting and fiscal management system, including level of pay and benefits

- Task orientation—emphasis placed on getting things done

- Professional orientation—emphasis placed on improving teaching and professional competence

In considering the fit between the individual and your center, you'll first want to explore the philosophical characteristics and unique culture of your center. Early childhood programs are social systems that reflect their own unique shared value systems and culture. When directors hear teachers report to each other, "We don't do that in our program," they are hearing something about the center's culture and philosophical characteristics.

Sometimes these characteristics reflect the values and beliefs of the dominant culture of the geographic area or region. Sometimes the social system within a center is a blend of characteristics, values, and beliefs from many cultures represented in the system. Components of the educational philosophy and culture within a school might include beliefs about how children learn, expectations for everyday demeanor, expectations of how to handle children's inappropriate behavior, and expectations for how to handle differences among co-workers.

Many of the characteristics that make centers unique are not explicit—they are subtle or unexpressed but present nevertheless. You may have to work to figure out and identify some of the more subtle aspects of your program that are critical determinants in maximizing the fit for prospective candidates. Investing the time to consider what makes your program unique, however, will pay off in determining your expectations for applicants and whether applicants are compatible with these expectations. A clear understanding about the unique cultural and programmatic components of your program will be a powerful contribution to the success of your recruitment and selection process.

Let's explore some dimensions of your program that reflect its unique character and consider some examples of how you might develop criteria to maximize the fit between a prospective candidate and your center.

Educational philosophy. Every program has an educational philosophy. In some programs, philosophies are written down, understood, and embraced by all. When this is the case, we say there is strong goal consensus—people agree on what they hope to achieve in their work with young children. In other programs, philosophies are less definitive, less clearly understood. If your program has a written philosophy, use it in figuring out the fit criteria for teachers who will be a good match with your center's approach in providing early care and education. If you don't have a written philosophy, you may want to begin working with your staff to write one.

Fit criteria related to educational philosophy will help you find applicants who share your view of the early childhood education landscape and are interested in teaching in ways that are compatible. For example, if your program values observing children at play as a source of emergent curriculum ideas, you will want

We don't see things as they are; we see things as we are.

Anaïs Nin

to find a candidate who understands this view and knows how to observe children at play to identify curriculum interests. It might also be important to find an applicant who has had experience in planning emergent curriculum. Such fit criteria will ensure that you do not end up selecting someone to join your staff who believes in predetermined, commercial curriculum as the preferred approach to curriculum planning.

Fit criteria for this example might be

- Capitalizes on children's interests to build curriculum
- Uses regular observation of children at play to identify interests
- Demonstrates the ability to identify children's interests from observation and to plan emergent curriculum based on those interests

Another aspect of educational philosophy is the role of the teacher. Your center's view of the teacher's role is a great place to look for fit criteria. Teachers perform many roles as they teach, and programs usually value a particular collection of philosophy-compatible roles. For example, if your program is a parent cooperative that staffs classrooms with one trained early childhood teacher and one parent volunteer, you will want to make sure that applicants understand the difference in the teaching role and the support role. Or if your program has a particular view of the teaching role as encompassing both direct instruction and play-based experiences, then use this particular point of view as the source of your fit criteria.

The goal in considering the role of the teacher is to confirm that the expectations in your program are a good fit with the teaching role expectations of applicants. The greater the clarity in your role expectations, the greater the chance that a new teacher will approach his or her job from a compatible perspective.

Fit criteria for this example might be

- Understands how to use volunteers as assistant teachers
- Embraces the role of facilitator as integral to teaching
- Uses direct instruction to scaffold children's interests during play
- Knows how to combine direct instruction with play-based experiences initiated and directed by the child

Co-worker relations. Programs have different expectations about peer relationships among staff. Some programs expect high levels of collegial interaction between teachers. They want teachers to collaborate, share and exchange ideas, support one another, and mentor emerging skills in novice colleagues. Other programs view the classroom as the teacher's professional domain where he or she is free to fulfill duties minimal input or interference from others. These different expectations will result in different fit criteria. Applicants who want many mentors and friends at work will be looking for something very different in a program from those who expect to be left alone to figure things out on their own.

Fit criteria for this example might be

- Works to resolve differences with colleagues in a direct and respectful way
- Supports collegial relationships between teachers by mentoring, observing, consulting, and reflecting with teaching peers
- Works independently to implement the curriculum and resolve classroom management issues

Leadership and management style. Center directors are integral to the smooth functioning of any program. Your philosophy of leadership and the repertoire of skills you use to manage your center impact many dimensions of your program, including how decisions are made, problems are solved, and supervision and performance appraisals are handled. Your leadership and management style impact the level of communication and information sharing that takes place between managers and staff. All are rich sources of fit criteria.

Finding fit criteria in this area is usually easy for experienced directors. They have insight into the type of staff members with whom they have had success in the past. New directors may not be able to identify these leadership characteristics so easily. A good place to start is looking at the teachers in your program with whom you have a good working relationship. Fit criteria will likely surface as you analyze why you are successful with these teachers. If you lead by example, expecting teachers to understand and model your behavior, you will want to find applicants who are best led by example. On the other hand, if your leadership style is more inspirational, you will want to find applicants who are motivated to do good work when their leaders inspire them.

Fit criteria for this example might be

- Integrates examples modeled by others into own teaching repertoire
- Focuses on goals set by supervisors and others
- Is empowered by inspirational leadership

Leadership and management styles are highly personal. Styles may be participatory or hierarchical, formal or informal. A director who likes autonomous, independent staff is less likely to successfully manage a teacher who needs lots of feedback and direction from her supervisor. Conversely, a director who expects teachers to follow her lead will want to make sure new teachers are willing to follow policies and procedures that are already set without venturing too far a field.

Fit criteria for this example might be

- Understands that decisions are made together by teachers and management
- Proceeds with solving problems without consultation from management
- Expects and embraces frequent feedback from supervising staff and management
- Follows standard operating policies and procedures when problems arise

Communication processes and conflict resolution. Every program has its own established patterns, both formal and informal, for communicating information. Developing fit criteria around this dimension is essential if a new employee is to transition smoothly into your program. For example, if your program relies heavily on written communication internally among staff and externally to parents and the community, you will need to develop fit criteria that stress this preference and skill set.

How are differences among staff or between staff and parents handled in your program? If your center has strong expectations for how problems and disagreements should be resolved, you will definitely want to establish some fit criteria to reflect your preferences. Disagreements can be solved in many ways. Some programs consider differences in the purview of the people involved. Other programs expect that management will be informed whenever minor or major disagreements surface. Thinking about how your program solves problems will help you develop appropriate fit criteria for conflict resolution.

Fit criteria for this example might be

- Creates win/win situations when problems arise
- Works to construct solutions to disagreements with others before involving management
- Maintains self-control, even when upset or angry

Parent relations. Central to successful family relations at any center is a shared understanding about the childrearing expectations of the families enrolled. These expectations contribute to the unique culture of any center. For example, whether or not families view children's independence as positive will influence the way the school views and incorporates teaching independence to individual children. This is not to say that there can't be differences in points of view on childrearing among teachers and between teachers and parents, but it does point to the importance of identifying the differences that might become criteria for maximizing the fit for potential applicants.

Most programs have guidance about parent relations in their philosophy statements—a good place to look for fit criteria in this area. But sometimes this is an area where guidance is implicit—unspoken or just assumed. Discussions with staff may uncover how the program actually responds or expects teachers to respond to parents in relation to this program characteristic.

Fit criteria for this example might be

- Demonstrates respect for all families from diverse cultures and backgrounds
- Works with parents to ensure compatible child guidance philosophies

Programs also have different approaches to the level of parent involvement desired. A clear understanding of your program's philosophy of family involvement and the teacher's role in making family participation happen is a critical area in developing fit criteria. For example, some programs welcome parents in the classroom in a variety of roles while others restrict visitation to certain times of the day or during certain activities. You will want to develop fit criteria to lead you in identifying the fit with applicants in this dimension of your program.

Fit criteria for this example might be

- Integrates many opportunities for parent involvement in the classroom
- Empowers parents and family members to be involved in the classroom and in contributing to their child's educational experience
- Coordinates parent involvement with other teachers and management to ensure continuity and consistency of programming

Physical environment and availability of resources. Teachers often complain that after they are hired they are surprised to discover how meager the equipment and supplies budget is to support them in creating an engaging classroom learning environment for their students. The situation poses a real hardship for those whose low salaries don't provide the cushion of extra spending money they need to buy odds and ends for their classroom. Clearly, an applicant who has a high need for ample teaching resources will perform better in programs where those resources are readily available. Assessing applicants' expectations regarding the physical environment, use of space, and allocation of resources for instructional materials is crucial for maximizing the fit.

Fit criteria for this example might be

- Follows procedures for ordering classroom supplies and materials
- Builds teaching resources by scrounging, recycling, and reusing materials

Identifying and Writing Fit Criteria

The process of identifying and writing criteria to maximize a good fit between the individual and the job and between the individual and your center can be formal or informal. You and your administrative staff can readily identify some criteria like start date, salary range, and general workload expectations. Other criteria, like previous experience required, preferred classroom management approach, or curriculum planning experience and expertise, can be identified in collaboration with your staff.

Take this opportunity to involve your staff in helping you really nail down the criteria that are most important and will increase the likelihood that the chosen candidate can succeed in his or her new job. As you do this, think carefully about those staff characteristics the individual must have as opposed to those that the individual might be able to learn on the job or acquire through training.

As you explore potential criteria to maximize the fit for a particular job within your program, it will be helpful to review the items listed on the three tables describing how people, jobs, and centers differ. Your criteria maximizing the fit between the person and the job and between the person and your center will ultimately be a unique blend of the elements on these three lists. Select dimensions from those listed that you feel communicate the most important fit criteria for your program. You can use the worksheet found in Appendix D to help you get started.

This is also a good time to take an inventory of the collective knowledge, skills, and expertise of staff. Are there any gaps? Use the opportunity of a job opening to develop specific fit criteria that will help fill gaps in specialized expertise. For example, if your staff has shown an interest in exploring the project approach and documentation, it makes sense to recruit someone who has experience in the project approach and can serve as a mentor and role model for teachers in learning more about the project approach and documentation methods.

Often, the opportunity to fill a vacancy is an opportunity to complement the strengths or balance the weaknesses of the teaching staff in your program. If you have teachers who are weak in curriculum planning, it is wise to look for a teacher with greater depth and experience in this area. If you have a highly experienced and seasoned staff, it might be a good time to hire a young, less experienced teacher who could benefit from strong mentors.

Criteria to complement staffs' strengths and weaknesses are likely to change often and vary for different positions. This is one area that you will need to reconsider each time you have a vacancy to ensure that the fit criteria you are using matches the current needs of your program or the specific needs of the position for which you are recruiting.

Whenever possible, write criteria in performance-based language—describe what teachers need to know, understand, and be able to do. Using this approach focuses your criteria on qualities you can measure, like a person's knowledge, understanding, skills, and abilities. This will increase the chance that you will find the right fit instead of just the right answers to your interview questions.

Performance-Based Words for Fit Criteria

Administers	Empowers	Oversees
Analyzes	Evaluates	Plans
Anticipates	Explains	Prepares
Applies	Focuses	Presents
Builds	Identifies	Records
Comprehends	Implements	Reviews
Constructs	Interprets	Summarizes
Coordinates	Integrates	Supplies
Constructs	Involves	Supports
Decides	Knows	Teaches
Designs	Links	Understands
Discusses	Maintains	Uses

Once you and your staff determine the appropriate criteria, they become a blueprint for exploring the closeness of fit with applicants. Interviewing and screening proceeds based on exploring and confirming the applicant's fit with the specific job you are filling and the applicant's fit with your program. Taken together, these criteria will be your guide in finding the candidate with the greatest chance of succeeding on the job.

CHAPTER 4

Interviewing and Screening Candidates

Your job announcement has been posted at a local community college, you've placed an ad in the newspaper, you've called your network of professional contacts, and you've carefully developed criteria that will help you determine the best fit between an applicant, the job, and your center. You are now ready to launch the next step in the recruitment process—interviewing and screening prospective candidates.

The interviewing and screening process detailed in this chapter includes several steps. The process begins by selecting a team to interview applicants. The team then designs an interview plan and screens applications to determine whom to invite for interviews. Next they plan for the actual interviews by carefully developing a protocol of questions and activities to assess competence. Finally, they schedule and conduct the interviews. There is no doubt that the effort put into this stage of recruitment is considerable. But the investment of time will definitely pay off later in successful integration and retention of the new hire.

In the preliminary phase of the recruitment process you (and perhaps one or two others on your administrative team) have done most of the work. Now as you enter the interviewing and screening phase of the process, you have the opportunity to expand participation to others on your staff—those teachers and support personnel who have a vested interest in a successful outcome.

Teachers Want More Involvement

Research indicates that teachers want to be more involved in the decision-making process for issues that directly affect them. One of those issues is the selection of colleagues. Co-worker relations are paramount when it comes to creating a nurturing early childhood environment. How compatible teachers are and how they interact with one another greatly influences the overall quality of your program. When teachers are involved in and contribute to the process of staff selection, it provides them with influence over something that is truly important to them.

Now is the time to make opportunities available to teachers who are ready to contribute to the interviewing and screening process. As you read this chapter, think about the different ways that interested teachers can participate. Some opportunities will be introductory—first steps in joining in. Others will require more commitment and expertise. No doubt about it, involving staff in helping you determine which applicant is the best fit for your program is complicated and time consuming. In the process, however, you are building goal consensus, nurturing collegiality, and encouraging greater commitment to a shared vision—important characteristics of centers with successful staff retention.

Some staff may feel they are not knowledgeable or skilled enough to participate in the interviewing and screening process. You can help them learn what they need to know by having them shadow more experienced teachers or by providing training. Either way, adding this important classroom perspective enriches the process and usually the outcome.

Responding to Initial Calls

A prospective candidate's first contact with your center is often by telephone. This initial contact is important. The applicant forms an impression of you and your center, and you form an initial impression of the applicant. Convincing each qualified applicant to submit an application is one of your goals in this initial contact. That is why it is so important to make a good impression. Briefly share information about the unique features of your school, what type of employee you are looking for, and why your program is a good place to consider for employment.

If you will not be handling initial inquiries yourself, it is best to designate just one or two others to perform this function. Make sure they are knowledgeable about the position and project a friendly, professional tone. Also make sure they do not engage in discussions with potential applicants that suggest your center prefers or will exclude a candidate on the basis of a protected employment status such as age, sex, race, marital status, and so on. Further, during the initial inquiry, a potential applicant may reveal that he or she will need a reasonable accommodation during the interviewing process or to perform the essential functions of the job if hired. Your staff members must be trained to forward this type of issue to you so that you can make sure you comply with and follow employment and labor laws. Investing time in training staff how to handle initial contacts helps ensure that no applicant drops your center from consideration because of ill feelings aroused during the initial contact.

At the same time, you don't want the telephone call to turn into a full-fledged interview. It is a time to encourage each caller to complete and submit an application so that his or her credentials can be compared to those required for the position and a determination made as to whether to invite the applicant for an interview. If contacts come in through other mechanisms like e-mail, fax, or post, respond as quickly to each one as you would to a telephone call, getting an application out to the inquirer as soon as possible.

Getting Comparable Information on Each Applicant

It is important to get consistent, comparable information from each applicant. The easiest way to do this is to have every candidate complete a standard employment application, whether or not they provide a resume or other written materials. This helps organize the basic information in a format that is easily compared among candidates. Most applications contain the following information:

- Personal information (name, address, contact numbers)

- Education

- Specialized training (for example, CDA, first aid certification, Montessori certification, infant/toddler certificate, director credential, state teacher certification)

- Job history and experience (most recent first)

- Professional memberships, awards and other honors

- References with addresses and contact numbers

Appendix E provides a template for an application form. Enlarge and add your school's logo. As applications are received, you can involve interested staff in making sure comparable information is received and highlighting information that is still needed.

Selecting the Interview Team

Think carefully about who will participate in the interviewing and screening process and the role that each team member will play. Some centers use the same interviewing team for all job vacancies so there is a consistent approach across hiring. Other programs rotate team members, including only those who are most vested in the hiring decision.

You can implement a model that has a few members involved in interviewing all positions and a few rotating members. For example, if you are recruiting a teacher with the ability to become an afternoon supervisor, the person to whom this position will report might be added to the team to assess the leadership and managerial abilities of applicants. Or if an experienced teacher has a co-teacher vacancy in her classroom, you will want to make sure that she is a member of the interview team. The decision about whom to hire is too important for her to not be included.

Keep the number of members on each team small enough to be efficient, yet large enough to voice different points of view about applicants. Three to five people should be adequate. For teachers who are not yet ready to assume full responsibility on the interview team, many participation opportunities are still available. These options will become clear as you design your interview plan.

When you select the people who will be on the interview team and establish some basic ground rules for how the group will proceed, be sure to clarify the scope of the responsibility and the issues of confidentiality. Will the team be making a recommendation to you as the director about whom to hire—in other words, ranking their preferred candidates and leaving the final decision to you? Or will they actually be deciding whom to hire? The first approach is a consultative model of decision making; the second is a delegated model. One approach isn't necessarily better than the other. Which one you choose depends on the experience level of the team and their interest and personal investment in making the final hiring decision. Be clear from the start about which approach you are using, however, so the team members understand the limits and scope of their decision-making authority. To understand more about shared decision making, read *Circle of Influence: Implementing Shared Decision Making and Participative Management*, another of the books in the Director's Toolbox Management Series.

Designing an Interview Plan

An important decision is which components you will use in the interview process for each job vacancy. What paperwork will you require from each applicant? Will you ask applicants for writing samples? Will you require peer interviews? Will you ask applicants to observe the classrooms? Will candidates do a teaching demonstration? At what point in the screening process will you contact references? The interview plan is designed to answer these and other questions. Consider the following range of possibilities as you construct the plan that will work for you and the job vacancy you seek to fill.

Writing samples. Writing samples serve multiple purposes. They convey information about the candidate's philosophy and approach to early care and education and provide insight into literacy levels. By requiring candidates to respond to a few of the interview questions in writing, you will be able to judge their ability to write clearly and express their thoughts and ideas cogently. For candidates who are not comfortable with oral interviews, writing samples provide a different way to assess their level of competence. Typically, the questions asked in writing samples are designed to elicit thoughtful answers. For example, *What are your career goals? What is the appropriate role of the teacher in the classroom?* If a writing sample is required as part of your interviewing process, be sure to let candidates know ahead of time.

Formal and informal assessments. Assessments can be commercially produced, standardized measures or informal questionnaires you develop for your center. For example, some programs require applicants to take a basic skills test to assess general competency in reading and numeration. Make certain that any such test has been validated to ensure that it does not have an adverse impact on a protected employment status (for example, a particular race or sex). Other assessments such as the Professional Activities Questionnaire and the Beliefs and Values Questionnaire (Appendices B and C) can be used to assess the candidate's fit with your organization. If an assessment will be used as part of the interviewing process, be sure to let candidates know ahead of time.

Peer interviews. Peer interviews are face-to-face conversations between teachers and the applicant. Peer interviews can be done individually, in pairs, or in a small group. Teachers who elect to participate in peer interviews will need mentoring to prepare for the experience. Peer interviews are the perfect place to use some of the fit criteria that you and your staff have developed. The process of developing criteria helps teachers assess their personal educational priorities and achieve goal consensus with their colleagues. A good list of questions derived from the fit criteria allows teachers to go into the interview with an agenda that is personally meaningful.

Center tour. Take candidates on a tour of your center. Seeing the physical facility and the program in action help applicants get an idea of how your program looks and operates. Tours can be brief, giving a glimpse rather than a complete view. The tour can also take place at various times during the interview process.

Serving as the tour guide is a good task for teachers who want to participate in the interviewing process but are not yet ready to take a more formal role. Teachers who take applicants on a tour are sharing the point of view of a classroom teacher—allowing the applicant to see the school from a potential colleague's point of view rather than that of an administrator. It also allows the teacher to get an impression of the applicant that can be added to the big picture later. Of course, teachers who give tours will need to be trained on appropriated and inappropriate topics for discussion with the applicant.

Classroom observation. Face-to-face interviewing can only get at some fit criteria. Give applicants a chance to observe a classroom in action. Observation helps candidates understand what the job is really like. It gives them a snapshot of the dynamics of the classroom and an opportunity to picture themselves in the classroom on the job. When the observation takes place before peer interviewing, it allows the peer interviewer to draw on the experience for further discussion. When observation occurs after the peer interview, the applicant can see how the teacher puts the center's philosophy into practice.

Timing of the observation is important. Naptime and lunchtime are probably not optimal. Choose relaxed, unhurried times of the day when children are at play, either indoors or outdoors. Make sure to communicate how long the observation will last so the candidate allows enough time at the interview. Also, share any ground rules or other expectations your program may have for observers.

Participation or demonstration teaching. Some programs require applicants to spend some time in the classroom in structured participation and/or demonstration. Adding this component to your interview plan allows teachers to observe candidate's skills in action. Participation can take place on the same day as peer interviews and observation or separately. It may be best to require only the final candidates to take on the role of active participant.

Plan for the participation or demonstration. Without a plan, the applicant won't know what to do and the teacher won't necessarily be able to transition to a meaningful activity at the spur of the moment. Help teachers think through what the applicants can do and what those tasks will reveal. Should the applicants read a story to a small group of children? Change the diaper of a child who allows strangers to do so? Participate with children in a small-group activity? Work with children on an art project? The candidate and teacher's advance preparation is necessary to make this a meaningful opportunity for evaluating the individual.

Not all teachers feel comfortable having applicants participate in their classrooms. Select teachers who are ready for this level of involvement in the interview process, helping them gain skills in observing and summarizing their impressions and evaluating the applicant's experience.

After the participation, make sure the teacher documents his or her impressions and writes an evaluation of the experience focusing on objective impressions (for example, the teaching behaviors observed) rather than subjective impressions. Ask teachers for feedback on specific work-related personality characteristics (tone of voice and sense of enthusiasm), interaction skills (reaction to children's approach and questioning skill), management skills (maintaining control and using positive discipline approaches), instructional skills (active engagement or adjusting the activity to the children's response), and any other teaching characteristics, skills, and abilities determined by your staff to be appropriate fit criteria for the job and for the center.

Portfolio review. Portfolios offer another source of information about a candidate, particularly about his or her view of important professional experiences. Professional portfolios are increasingly a part of professional preparation programs, so many of the candidates who have attended college will be eager to submit their professional portfolios with their resume. It is important to decide if you will review portfolios and how you will ensure that the portfolio review adds information to the interview process. Some portfolios are nothing more than collections of class assignments from college courses. How will you handle these? If some applicants have portfolios and others don't, will the portfolio be used in the decision-making process?

Consider ways to include a review of at least some portfolio entries in your interview process. You might ask applicants to select two or three portfolio entries that best reflect your fit criteria, like their experience, their curriculum planning skills, or their guidance strategies. Used this way, information from portfolios can add to the information collected in the interview process.

Evaluating portfolios provides another way to get teachers involved. You might offer teachers who have completed their own professional portfolios an opportunity to look at those shared by applicants, adding a new point of view to the interview data gathered.

These are typical strategies used in the interview process. Which options you select are less important than having a good variety of information-gathering strategies that elicit a well-rounded view of the candidate and different points of view from your interview team. With this range of information and viewpoints, you are more likely to come to the right conclusion about the fit between each candidate's skills and abilities and the available job.

Conducting a Preliminary Screening of Applications

Your goal in this step of the recruitment process is to determine whom to interview—which applicants deserve serious consideration. Develop a strategy that helps you approach screening systematically and allows you to quickly check to see if the applicants meet the fit criteria set forth in your job description. Then assess whether you have the necessary materials to proceed. A form that parallels the application form completed by each applicant can be used to record the information you have collected so far. As you review the application, jot down questions to ask in the interview about inconsistencies, incomplete answers, or interesting information.

During this initial screening, look for the following:

- Appearance of the application: Is all of the information complete? Is it signed, giving you permission to check references?

- Missing information in the candidate's summary of professional experiences: Are there any blanks? Are there gaps in the information?

- Reasons for job changes: Do the job changes detailed on the application seem logical? Are they consistent with other information the candidate has provided?

- Career progression: Do job changes represent growth in income or in responsibility? Does your job opportunity fit into the applicant's growth pattern?

- Match with your center's fit criteria: Does the information detailed on the application indicate that the candidate will be a good match for the requirements of the job and the needs of the center?

For applicants meeting the job requirements, conduct an initial reference check. Use the initial reference check to ascertain the accuracy and validity of the application information. Request confirmation that the information provided on the application, like hire dates, salary history, longevity in each position, is correct. An initial reference check may also be used to get information about the correct person to talk to later about the candidate's on-the-job performance. By conducting an initial reference check at this stage in the interviewing and screening process, you may get valuable information that you'll want to explore in greater depth during the interview. You can do a more thorough reference check of the candidate later on, during the final selection phase. Appendix F is a form you can use for your initial screening.

Confirming this information before the interview allows the interview team to discuss discrepancies with the applicant during the interview. It also gives the team valuable insight into which areas to explore further in the interview. For example, if an applicant's salary history indicates that her ending salary is higher than the salary range for the position for which he or she is applying, salary should be discussed early in the interview process to determine the compatibility of the applicant with your organization.

Planning Your Interview Protocol

A good interview team will plan each interview in advance, using the same general format for all applicants. This makes evaluations between candidates easier. Having a plan keeps the interview focused, prevents the team members from repeating questions, and helps ensure that pertinent information is gathered while the applicant is present. Preparing carefully for interviews increases the likelihood that the process will end in a successful hire for the program. Preparation begins by reviewing each application carefully, identifying good interview questions, avoiding common interview mistakes, and structuring the experience to make applicants feel comfortable and at ease.

All the work you and your staff put into identifying criteria to maximize the fit between the individual, the job, and your center will be used now to ensure that you find the right person from the applicant pool. Here is an example of how different approaches can be used to gather data about one fit criteria.

The closest to perfection a person ever comes is when he fills out a job application form.

Stanley J. Randall

Integrating Fit Criteria into the Interview Plan			
Example of fit criteria	**How investigated?**	**Question to ask**	**Person responsible**
Demonstrates respect for all families including those from diverse cultures and backgrounds	In interview	"Share some of the curriculum ideas and instructional strategies you've used to demonstrate respect for families from diverse cultures."	Director
	Look at portfolio	"Does your portfolio address how you worked with diverse cultures?"	Peer interviewer
	Ask supervisor	"How did this applicant work with families from diverse backgrounds?"	Director
	Discuss when talking about philosophy	"How do you handle holiday celebrations in your classroom?"	Peer interviewer

Information gleaned from the candidate's application and the fit criteria you have developed with your staff should be the source of your interview questions.

Review the applications to identify questions to ask the applicant. Look for the following to uncover experiences reported by the applicant that may require further investigation:

- Gaps in employment

- Job history—length of time in previous employment; short-term and sequential jobs; long stretches of unrelated work; too much personal information; lack of detail about former employers

- Experience—variety, with what age groups, in what kinds of settings

- Knowledge—gained formally and informally, credentials that validate knowledge and skills, unique experiences that indicate elevated competence and expertise in an area

- Insights into personal strengths; areas for further growth and development

The following table provides an example of questions that might be prompted by review of a candidate's job application and resume.

Constructing Interview Questions for a Teacher Position	
Example of questions	**To discover information about**
Tell me about the classes in college you enjoyed the most.	School experience
In which subjects were you strongest? In which subjects did you make the highest (lowest) grades?	The kind of effort the candidate invested in school
Describe the jobs you held during college.	College job experiences and their applicability to the current job opportunity
How did you select your first employer?	Job search strategies
Who was your immediate supervisor?	Confirm or expand reference contacts
What were your greatest satisfactions (frustrations) in that job?	Indicators of satisfaction/stress
How long did it take you to ... • feel comfortable in your first/last job? • plan curriculum for your classroom? • get to know the parents of the children?	Response to change and time-management skills
Tell me about the characteristics of your favorite (least favorite) supervisor.	Experiences with previous supervisors, supervisory expectations
What do you want a supervisor to do to support you as a teacher?	Potential matches or mismatches with supervisory styles
What were you were doing from ____ to ____?	Gaps in employment

Which job was most satisfying to you? Why? Which job was least satisfying to you? Why?	Job history; length of time in previous employment; short-term and sequential jobs; long stretches of unrelated work; lack of details about previous employers
In your last teaching job, tell me about your most rewarding experiences regarding ... • parent relationships • curriculum • co-worker relations	Previous experience; details and successes in previous experiences
In your last teaching job, tell me how you handled ... • aggression • biting • parent complaints • conflict with co-workers	Ability to reflect on previous experience; different strategies used
How do you identify ideas for an emergent curriculum? How do you individualize for different developmental levels?	Measure or confirm knowledge and skills
What are the characteristics you liked in your colleagues? What characteristics bothered you?	Identify personality characteristics that are desirable to the applicant Determine characteristics that may create conflict with current staff personalities.
What do you see yourself doing in five years? Are you satisfied with your career path so far? Does your current employer know that you are looking to move?	Insight into profession goals Satisfaction with progress toward goals Approach to changing jobs—sharing that with employer or not?

Write out the questions so the interview team has them during the actual interview. As you refine the wording of each question make sure it elicits the kind information you need. Use behavior-based questions that focus on past behavior, not hypothetical situations. For example, "Tell me about a time when you ..." "Describe how you go about ..." Structure questions carefully so that interviewees don't give socially desirable responses. Open-ended questions serve this purpose better than closed questions. Here are examples of some good interview questions you might ask.

Interview Questions

- If you were choosing a center for your child, what would you look for?

- What is the most important quality you have to offer children?

- Describe your special talents and skills.

- What professional accomplishment are you most proud of?

- Describe the ideal teacher for young children.

- Why are you interested in working for this center?

- Describe a mentor you've had. How did that person help you grow professionally?

- What was your worst work experience? Why?

- How do you respond to a mother who asks you to make sure her child never cries?

- How would your co-workers at your last job describe you?

- What do you like to do for relaxation?

- Describe a situation where you planned an activity for young children that didn't work out. What did you learn from the experience?

- When a child refuses to eat, what do you do?

- How do you think children should be toilet trained?

- How do you feel about changing diapers or cleaning up after a sick child?

- If a parent asked you to suggest a good children's book, what would you recommend? Why?

- What do you do when a child cries for his parents when they leave? What if the crying persists for weeks?

- If a child hits you, what do you do?

- What is your fondest [worst] memory about childhood?

- Describe a situation where you had a conflict with one of your co-workers. How did you handle the situation?

- Give some examples of how you organize your personal and professional life to get everything done.

- What are your favorite children's books for this age level?

- What strategies would you use to train a classroom aide with no experience?

- What role does customer service play in early care and education?

- What are the specific things you do to establish rapport with parents?

- Describe a time in a previous job when you felt you were treated unfairly. What did you do about it?

- What can teachers do to improve society's view of early childhood education?

- What new professional skills are you eager to learn?

- What book has been influential in shaping your philosophy and beliefs about being a teacher of young children?

- If you had a role in selecting your co-workers, what qualities would you look for?

- Describe your best day at your last job.

Keep in mind as you develop your interview questions that there are questions you cannot ask due to federal and state employment discrimination laws. The Equal Employment Opportunity Commission (EEOC) provides guidelines to help you avoid discriminatory hiring practices. Individual states have additional restrictions. The guiding principle is that questions asked of applicants must have a "business necessity." It is always a good idea to have your program's attorney or human resources consultant review your list of interview questions to make sure that you are not asking questions that violate these laws. In general, here are some of the questions you cannot ask.

Questions that directly or indirectly inquire about ...

- age, race, color, ancestry, or national origin

- marital status, dependents, child care arrangements, or housing arrangements

- whether or not the applicant is pregnant

- arrest and/or conviction records, except those required by law

- health status and history

- type of military discharge or veteran's status

- willingness to work extended hours or on weekends (unless specified in the job description and advertisements)

- union memberships/affiliations

- gender-specific information that would not be asked of all applicants (like who takes your children to school or what role your spouse plays in your household)

- disabilities of either the applicant or his/her family members

- family information—number of children, spouse's employment

- workers' compensation record/history

- religion (unless your center is a private, religion-affiliated institution)

- statuses that are protected by your state, county, or local laws. These may include such things as sexual orientation, height and weight, genetic background, parental status, or HIV status

There are topics where you need to word your questions carefully. For example, you may not ask a person's religious affiliation, but you can ask if the scheduled workdays are suitable. Likewise, while you may not ask if the person has a physical disability, it is appropriate and lawful to ask if the person can perform the specific job functions as described in the job description. Further, if the job has particular physical requirements, you may ask the candidate to demonstrate how he or she would meet those requirements so long as you ask every candidate to demonstrate those physical abilities and not simply the candidates who are disabled or look weak.

Remember not to reject a disabled candidate out of hand simply because he or she cannot perform a physical or other task unassisted. The Americans with Disabilities Act and its state law counterparts require that employers provide a reasonable accommodation to qualified disabled individuals to enable them to perform a job. If a candidate does or may have a disability, you may want to consult with an employment attorney or legal aid organization to ensure that you comply with ADA guidelines.

As you develop your interview protocol, make sure to build in opportunities for reciprocity. Encourage applicants to ask questions often during the interview process and provide opportunities for applicants to gather their own information about the position as they spend time with the interview team members. Remember, if your goal is to determine the fit between applicants and your program, you need to have a clear understanding of the applicants' perceptions of the work environment they are looking for to promote their own professional fulfillment. You want candidates who are as particular about the place they work for as you are about the people you hire. Maximizing the fit is a two-way process.

You also need to decide who will conduct each part of the interview, which fit criteria will be investigated during each component of the interview process, who will investigate it, and how to go about getting the information. When your plan is this detailed, you are guaranteed to have a great deal of usable data to refer to during the selection process.

Scheduling and Conducting Interviews

Earlier in this chapter, you learned about the possible components of an interview plan. As you plan the actual interview, you need to decide just how much time to allot to each component. The following table presents a time-flow sequence of activities for both a one-day interview and a two-day interview.

Interview conducted in one day

Greeting and introductions (10 minutes)

⇨ candidate completes assessments and writing sample (15 minutes)

⇨ initial interview (30 minutes)

⇨ center tour (10 minutes)

⇨ classroom observation (30 minutes)

⇨ peer interviews (15 - 30 minutes)

⇨ demonstration teaching (15 - 30 minutes)

⇨ portfolio review (10 minutes)

⇨ summary interview (15 minutes).

Interview conducted over two days

First visit:

Greeting and introductions (10 minutes)

⇨ candidate completes assessments and writing sample (15 minutes)

⇨ initial interview (45 minutes)

⇨ classroom observation (30 minutes)

⇨ center tour (15 minutes)

⇨ summary interview (15 minutes).

Second visit:

Demonstration teaching (15 - 30 minutes)

⇨ peer interviews (15 - 30 minutes)

⇨ portfolio review (10 minutes)

⇨ summary interview (15 minutes).

In good job markets, applicants often have more than one interview scheduled. Take this into consideration in timing the interview. You want to be able to pursue an applicant through the interview process without losing him or her to another employer. If your procedures are too cumbersome or time consuming, the applicant may make a decision about employment before you finish the interviewing process. This does not mean that the process should be compromised; just consider the length of time an applicant may be in the market and adjust your interview plan accordingly. Condense or shorten steps if you feel an applicant is highly qualified and desirable.

When you have identified how long each interview component will take, it is time to schedule applicants for interviews. Make a schedule that gives the interview team time to conduct thorough interviews and ensures that each applicant gets the attention he or she deserves. Plan sufficient break time between the end of one interview and the beginning of another so that candidates are not kept waiting and the interview team does not feel rushed.

"I see by your résumé that you don't stay in one place very long."

©Bunny Hoest. Reprinted with permission.

Following your interview schedule, invite applicants for interviews. Tell applicants how much time they should allow for the interview and what to anticipate. Information about writing samples, classroom observation and participation, demonstration teaching, peer or group interviews, and the approximate time allotted for each step should be shared at this time.

If you view the interviewing process through the lens of public relations, you will want to make sure you are well prepared before your candidate arrives. You and your team should have a clear sense of the interviewing protocol and will have reviewed your role responsibilities. Whether or not you ultimately end up hiring a particular candidate, you want to have the individual leave with a good impression of your center.

Think carefully about where you will conduct interviews. The room should be free of distractions and all parties should be able to hear one another easily. Ensure that the seating is comfortable. Try to avoid an arrangement of tables and chairs that makes candidates feel like they are at an inquisition. Friendly but professional is the order of the day.

A successful interview begins with making applicants feel comfortable. Start by being a gracious host. Offer water, coffee, tea, or a cold drink. Social pleasantries like this give the applicant time to settle down and get a feel for how things will proceed. Manners count—always start your interview on time.

Use the applicant's name as you talk. In fact, you might start by asking for the correct pronunciation of the applicant's name and how he or she likes to be addressed. Then match your level of formality to the level that makes the applicant comfortable. For example, if the applicant asks to be called Mrs. Garcia, then use her surname, Mrs. Garcia, instead of her first name. Make eye contact as you settle in, commenting on how stressful interviews can be and acknowledging that the candidate might be nervous or anxious. Use reflective listening techniques to confirm if your identification of feelings is accurate or not.

Start the interview with a few general, nonthreatening questions to help the applicant relax and feel comfortable. Some examples might be, "Did you have any trouble finding our school?" "How did you find out about this job opportunity?" Asking applicants how they learned about the job opening also offers clues about which recruitment strategies are working. Then explain the interview plan—what will happen during the applicant's time with you. Tell the applicant why the job is vacant (for example, an expansion position, promotion of teacher, resignation, or termination). This gives the applicant some information about the situation and relieves anxiety about why the position is vacant.

With this introduction you are ready to carry out the interview protocol you have designed. During the face-to-face interview, pay attention to who is talking. You want the applicant to talk more than the interviewers. Remember also to take notes. Jot down notes about answers to questions rather than trying to write down every word.

Some Interviewing Mistakes to Avoid

- Failure to establish rapport and starting with questions that are threatening or too probing

- Talking too much, preventing the applicant from having a chance to respond to questions or bring up issues

- Failure to provide enough structure for the interview or letting the applicant go off on unrelated tangents

- Lack of follow-up on questions asked with reflective listening techniques and additional clarifying or expansion questions

- Asking leading questions requiring only a yes or no or to which the desired answer is readily apparent

- Stereotyping applicants based on information received in the application that limits the interviewer's ability to be objective and search out potential common ground

- Overlooking red flags or issues that need to be discussed because the interviewer's overall impression of the applicant is positive.

- Asking questions that are not business related, thereby eliciting answers that may reflect inappropriate personal information about age, marital issues, religion, medical concerns, or the like.

- Taking notes during the interview that reflect the interviewer's personal opinions rather than facts.

Take advantage of interviews to point out to the applicants some of the unique features or special advantages of employment at your school that they may not know. End interviews by asking candidates if there is any additional information they need to know about your center or the specific job. Close interviews by answering the applicant's questions. Then share your timeline for making a decision and how candidates will be informed of their status. Send the applicants away with a clear idea about what will happen next. Make sure they leave with your business card or information about how to contact you if they have questions.

Keeping track of the information collected during interviews is a challenge. It is estimated that half of the interview content is forgotten before the interview is over and as much as 85% is lost by the next day. Summarizing your notes immediately after an interview will help prevent "blending," where all candidate responses seem the same. Figure out a way to keep information from getting lost. Develop a form for recording notes that will prompt you to remember the details of the interview later. Appendix G is a sample form you might find useful as you summarize your impressions from the interview.

When interviews are well planned and carefully implemented, both you and the applicants will consider the experience worthwhile and informative regardless of who is selected. You will have the information you need to proceed to the next step of the recruitment process—selecting the applicant who is the right fit for your position and program. The candidate will leave with a positive impression of your center whether or not they ultimately come to work with you.

CHAPTER 5

Selecting the Right Candidate

If your initial advertising attracted a good pool of high-quality candidates to invite for interviews, you may be in the enviable position of having several individuals who the interview team believes would be a good fit for the job and your center. On the other hand, if the job market in your community is quite competitive, your interviewing and screening process may have surfaced only one or two individuals who the team feels are a good fit.

In either case, the final step of selecting the right candidate for the position needs to be handled carefully to ensure that you have covered all bases and are not making too hasty a decision based on incomplete information or sheer desperation to fill the vacancy. Being conscientious in documenting how decisions are made during this phase of the process will also help protect for your center from liability for alleged discrimination in the hiring process. This chapter looks at the importance of conducting a complete reference check on candidates and the range of issues you must consider as you make your offer of employment.

The Importance of Checking References

It has been said that past behavior is the best predictor of future behavior. If you agree with that pearl of wisdom, then you'll appreciate the importance of investing time to do a thorough background check on the candidates you are considering. This step in the recruitment and hiring process is crucial even if you or members of your team have had contact with the individual being considered in another context—for example, as a classmate in a college class or a fellow member on a committee in a civic organization.

LaShonda is the director of a corporate-sponsored child care program housed in a suburban corporate office complex. She is also a student in an early childhood degree program at the state university located in her city. During one of the sessions of her Early Childhood History and Philosophy class at the university, LaShonda distributes a job vacancy announcement for a lead teacher position open at her center. She is thrilled when one of her fellow students, Regina, expresses interest in applying for the position. She knows Regina is a very capable student, bright and articulate in class, and is confident she will connect well with the highly educated parent clientele her program serves. She is excited to think that Regina may become part of her teaching team.

The interview goes well. LaShonda involves two other teachers and the corporate liaison to participate in the interviews and observe Regina in action. All feedback from the other members of the team is positive. Because LaShonda feels she knows Regina well from being with her in class for a full semester, she reasons that it will not be necessary to do a reference check. The offer is extended. Regina accepts and starts her employment promptly.

LaShonda's hopes for a good fit quickly fade when she realizes Regina has a different concept of neatness than LaShonda and her staff. LaShonda's team prides themselves on the organized and neat physical appearance of their classrooms. They are very conscientious about picking up after themselves and putting things away. The parents and the corporate liaison that regularly visit the center reinforce this norm. Regina, on the other hand, is a die-hard clutter-bug, a real pack rat at heart.

Within two weeks of her hire, crates and boxes are piled everywhere. Within a month it is clear there is a real clash in Regina's definition of neat and the norms of the center. Gentle hints and reminders don't seem to work. It takes LaShonda three months before she finally confronts Regina about her messy classroom. Regina is offended that LaShonda characterizes her room as an "eye sore." The other teachers on the staff aren't so gracious in their descriptions, preferring instead to use words like "pig's sty." Tensions mount and within the year, Regina leaves the program feeling bitter.

As LaShonda reflects on lessons learned from this experience she regrets not having taken more time to find out from previous colleagues and employers about Regina's work style. This is clearly a strong criteria for fit within LaShonda's center and she totally missed it in the interviewing process.

To gather information about a candidate's previous work performance, you can conduct either a telephone reference check, a written check, or both. The goal of a reference check is to assess the previous employer's satisfaction with the employee, get another view of the applicant's skills and knowledge, and understand the applicant's unique experiences.

Before contacting previous employers or other references provided by a candidate, be sure to get the candidate's permission. The following is sample language you can include in your employee authorization to investigate. This release can be included at the end of your application form or as a separate document. Making this explicit with the candidate is important. It is particularly crucial if the candidate is still employed elsewhere and may not want the current employer to know about his or her job search. If your center does not undertake this investigation but rather engages an individual or entity outside your organization, this form will not be adequate and you will need to consult with legal counsel about procedures under the Fair Credit Reporting Act.

Authorization to Investigate Employment Application

I understand that a part of Hickory Woods Child Development Center's (the "Center") consideration of my application for employment, the Center may investigate my employment history, educational background, references, and certifications, as well as other information pertinent to my candidacy. I understand that the Center's inquiry may extend beyond verification of representations made by me, either written or oral, about my qualifications and that the Center may seek assessments of my character and fitness for employment by the Center.

I knowingly and without qualification authorize the Center to undertake such an investigation. In addition, I agree to hold harmless the Center, its employees, directors, officers, agents, successors, and assigns from any liability for any information that it may obtain, disclose, share or exchange during the course of its investigation. Further, I agree to hold harmless any individual and any entity and its employees, directors, officers, agents, successors, and assigns from any liability for any information that it may disclose, share or exchange with the Center in connection with the Center's investigation.

_____
Signature

_____
Printed name

_____
Date

Sometimes just mentioning that you intend to talk to a past employer will prompt candidates to share additional information about their previous work history that might not have come out in the interview or on their application. This is particularly true if they believe the individual you are contacting might not share favorable information.

In talking to previous employers or other professional references on the telephone, probe for information that will give you a fuller picture of the candidate, not just information confirming your initial impressions. Try to be as objective as possible, and don't be afraid to use silence to draw out information from the reference. Be sure to ask similar questions of each reference you contact so that the answers can be compared. You'll find the list of questions on page 71 helpful as you create your own list tailored to the position you are filling. End your discussion with the question, "Do you have anything else to add that would help us make an informed decision?"

As you construct your list of questions to ask previous employers and/or other professional contacts, be aware of the time required to answer those questions so that you do not unduly impose on the person. It takes time to give thoughtful responses. Don't rush the process. Assure the individual of the confidentiality of remarks.

Written reference checks can follow telephone checks. Written checks give contacts the opportunity to add to the snapshot of the applicant. Be sure to include a stamped, addressed envelope with the form you send and indicate the date you need the information returned. Include a space on your form where the respondent can describe how he or she feels about the candidate in more subjective terms. Appendix H is a sample of a reference form you can use for this purpose.

Some candidates will send written reference letters along with their resume when they apply for a position. You can be the judge of the value of these letters, but don't assume that they provide a full picture of the applicant's true abilities. Many employers discount letters submitted by the applicant as biased. Who would send a reference letter that wasn't flattering? On the other hand, if you have several letters, you may see a pattern of impressions emerge from the reference contacts that is helpful. To ensure that the reference provides you with the information you want to know instead of just what the candidate has chosen to submit, talk to those who have written references to get additional information.

Keeping track of information discussed in the telephone reference checks beyond a generally positive or negative reaction is a challenge. Make notes during the conversation and transfer all of the information you get to a standardized form so you can compare the references of all the people contacted.

- When did the candidate work for you? What dates?

- Does the following description accurately portray the responsibilities the candidate had while working for you? (Read the applicant's description of the job from his/her application.)

- Was the candidate's work attendance consistent? If not, how often was he or she absent? Did the candidate arrive at work on time?

- Was the candidate flexible and willing to go beyond the boundaries of his or her job description when needed?

- Tell me about the candidate's interactions with children. How does the candidate handle problem situations with children?

- Tell me about the candidate's ability to communicate and work with parents. How does the candidate handle a problem situation with a dissatisfied parent?

- How well did the candidate get along with his or her co-workers? Describe any problems there may have been with a co-worker. How did the candidate handle the situation?

- Describe any problems there were between the candidate and his or her supervisor. Was the candidate able to resolve these difficulties?

- What do you see as the candidate's strengths?

- What areas would you identify for professional growth for the candidate?

- Do you have any reservations about recommending the candidate for a position in the early care and education field?

- Would you rehire the candidate again?

- If the candidate was good at her job, what kept you from inducing her to stay?

- Is there any other information you would like to share that would be helpful in making our hiring decision?

Handling Reluctant References

Many employers have a blanket policy of only providing information about an employee's dates of employment and positions he or she has held. Understandably, they are reluctant to share additional information about former employees for fear of incurring legal liability. Others will furnish information only in writing. When this is the case, see if you can find out about additional contacts who would be willing to share more information. Ask for names of colleagues with whom the candidate worked. Often, it is necessary to identify the direct supervisor who has firsthand experience with the applicant and is able to comment on the former employee's experience and performance within the organization. If the person worked for a large agency, the human resources office is apt to only share hire and separation dates and positions held.

Sometimes people's reluctance to provide more than cursory information may be a clue in itself regarding their feelings about the candidate. Listen to the tone and tenor of how people comment on the applicant. Do their voices communicate enthusiasm about the person or are they cautious and guarded in how and what they say?

Remember, however, there are many reasons people leave one position and pursue another. You could have a stellar candidate who still gets a lousy reference from a previous employer. As the following vignette demonstrates, you need to make a judgment call in these instances about the veracity and source of the information.

Maria has just completed the interviewing process for a lead teacher position at her center. Her interview team is quite enthusiastic about Lauren, a soft-spoken, but articulate young woman in her late 20s. When Maria calls four of Lauren's references, including two past employers, she is perplexed that three of the four references share only glowing feedback about Lauren. They state that she was a "conscientious employee," "a creative and inspiring teacher," and a "deeply committed early childhood professional." The fourth reference, a man who owns a center where Lauren worked three years previously, refers to her as "haughty" and "undependable."

Maria cannot understand the discrepancy in feedback she has received about Lauren. In a follow-up conversation with Lauren, Maria, asks her an open-ended question. "How do you think your previous co-workers and employers would describe you?" Lauren hesitates a moment and then

Verifying Credentials

In addition to contacting previous employers and other professional references provided by the candidate, it is essential to verify the veracity of an individual's credentials as summarized in his or her job application or resume. The kinds of verification depends on the type of position you are filling. For example, you may only require teacher certification for certain positions at your center. Here are some general categories to think about.

Degrees, certificates, and credentials. In some cases a photocopy of a certificate of completion of a specialized training course or certification will suffice for verification of a candidate's credentials. This might include such things as certification in first aid and the Heimlich maneuver. For other certifications, such as a state teaching credential, you'll want the certificate registration number or a certified copy of the credential. In some instances you may want to have official transcripts sent directly from the college or institution conferring the degree or certificate. If the employee will be transporting children as part of their job, you'll also want to make sure you have a copy of his or her driver's license.

Employment eligibility verification. The Immigration and Nationalization Service of the Department of Justice provides a form for identifying employment eligibility to work. All employees are required to prove eligibility to work in this country. To be in compliance with the Immigration Reform and Control Act of 1986, every person hired by your center must complete Form I-9. This form is available from the Immigration and Naturalization Service (INS). Contact information for the INS is located in the reference section. You will need to have this completed as part of your employee intake process.

Criminal background check.   Most states have passed laws requiring a criminal background check for employees working in child care centers as part of compliance with P.L. 98-473.   Even if your state does not require it, a criminal background check is a critical way to help defend your center against a claim of negligent hire.   Contact your state's child care licensing division for information on procedures for securing a criminal background check on prospective employees.

Federal policies require that Head Start personnel sign a declaration prior to employment that lists all pending and prior criminal arrests and charges relating to child sexual abuse and their disposition, convictions related to other forms of child abuse and/or neglect, and all convictions of violent felonies.   This declaration does not automatically disqualify a person from being hired.   Head Start programs must review each case to assess the relevance of an arrest, charge, or conviction to a hiring decision.

Summarizing Information on Each Candidate

After interviews and reference checks are completed, it is time to summarize the information on each candidate for the team to review and make a hiring decision. A summary sheet will help ensure that you have all of the information you need and identify strengths, issues, questions, and concerns to be considered by the team.   The candidate's personal information that is not business related has no place in the selection process and no place on the summary sheet (or any other documentation of the selection process).   Make sure that all staff members who are involved, even tangentially, in the hiring process are trained to base their input on the questions and responses from the interview and their review of records, and to avoid speculation about a candidate's personal life.

It is also very important to continue to rate candidates against the objective criteria you have established, not against one another.   If you find as a team you must use a personal comparison, use someone who has successfully performed the job in the past.   The following summary sheet shows how one interview team organized its information on the three candidates it interviewed for a toddler teacher position.

Candidate: Marsha M.

Criteria	Interview team ratings				
	Pam	Lila	Roz	Jason	Total
Previous work experience	5	5	4	5	19
General and specialized education	4	3	3	4	14
Personal characteristics	4	4	3	5	16
Fit with the job	4	4	3	4	15
Fit with the center	4	5	4	5	18

Summary of strengths:	Summary of weaknesses:
— Great with musical activities	— Not willing to work morning shift
— Wonderful singing voice	— Was 10 minutes late for interview
— Gentle interactions with the children	
— Very patient	
— Good range of work experiences	
— Glowing references	

Candidate: Robyn W.

Criteria	Interview team ratings				
	Pam	Lila	Roz	Jason	Total
Previous work experience	4	4	5	4	17
General and specialized education	5	5	5	5	20
Personal characteristics	3	4	3	3	13
Fit with the job	3	3	4	4	14
Fit with the center	4	4	4	4	16

Summary of strengths:	Summary of weaknesses:
— Good energy level	— Harsh voice, poor diction
— Strong understanding of temperaments	— Changes jobs frequently
— Strong professional orientation	
— Wide range of experiences	
— Solid references	

Candidate: Liz B.

	Interview team ratings				
Criteria	Pam	Lila	Roz	Jason	Total
Previous work experience	2	2	1	2	7
General and specialized education	3	4	3	4	14
Personal characteristics	5	5	5	4	19
Fit with the job	4	4	4	3	15
Fit with the center	5	5	5	5	20

Summary of strengths:
— Very nurturing style with children
— Creative repertoire of art activities
— Willing to work any hours
— Good sense of humor
— Wants to write children's books someday
— Can draw cartoon figures

Summary of weaknesses:
— Dropped out of two college classes
— Not enthusiastic about outdoor play
   (doesn't like insects)
— This would be her first full-time job –
   only babysitting references

When summaries are complete, ask team members to review each file and rank the candidates. Independently ranking each applicant allows individual points of view to solidify. Then meet together to share rankings, discuss and review material, and make a group ranking of candidates. The group ranking may be the same as individual rankings or it may be different. The purpose of this step is to consider different points of view as a way of exploring candidate strengths and weaknesses and the fit between applicants and the job and center.

Using the strategy of developing specific criteria and summarizing individual team members' rankings as they relate to the criteria helps the group avoid the *halo effect*—letting one positive or negative characteristic of a candidate influence opinions about the overall appropriateness of the candidate. To keep this from happening, focus the team's discussions on the evidence they gathered in the interview, reference checks, and other components of the interview process.

Jason has worked for three years lining up the capital needed to design and build what he dreams will be a model child development center in an upper-middleclass community. When it looks like the construction will be completed on schedule, Jason begins in earnest his quest to find a first-class staff. He holds sole responsibility for recruiting, interviewing, and hiring. He posts recruitment ads at several colleges, persuades a columnist for a local newspaper to write a feature story about his new venture, and creates a display board to advertise positions at the state AEYC conference.

Jason aggressively courts the most talented preschool teachers he knows to join his start-up team. While the salaries he offers are not all that outstanding, Jason's enthusiasm about the new center when he talks with prospective candidates is contagious. In the end he has a large pool of highly qualified candidates from which to choose. Jason's strategy is straightforward—hire the best and the brightest! Out of 22 teachers, 5 have master's degrees and 11 have baccalaureate degrees. The remaining have associate's degrees. Jason is elated. He is sure his center will be a wonderful success.

Jason's bubble bursts by the time he celebrates the center's first anniversary. All but one of the teachers with master's degrees has left employment and five of the teachers with baccalaureate degrees have left. His turnover rate is over 40% in his first year of operation. In reflecting back on his hard-learned lessons, Jason says, "I was so naïve. My strategy was so short sighted. I didn't think about the long-term needs of the center. I hired solely on the basis of paper qualifications, not people's growth potential. After the initial enthusiasm of working in a new center wore off, the reality of the low salaries coupled with the lack of promotion opportunities caused an absolute tidal wave of resignations. I think if I had just involved more people in the hiring and interviewing process, I wouldn't have been so narrow in my focus on paper qualifications."

Look for patterns of evidence from different sources. For example, if the candidate's classroom participation or demonstration teaching were inadequate, look for other evidence of inadequate performance from references, short-term employment, or lack of educational attainment. If none of these sources of evidence are consistent with the candidate's performance during the demonstration teaching, there may be another explanation for the inadequate performance. Perhaps the candidate was nervous or the teacher who set up the participation wasn't prepared. In this case, another participation session might be in order to give the candidate a chance to demonstrate his or her skills. Don't hesitate to gather more information to assist with your decision.

The Ethics of Selection

The *Code of Ethical Conduct and Statement of Commitment* developed by the National Association for the Education of Young Children (NAEYC) provides guidelines for responsible behavior in early childhood educators. Several of these guidelines apply to making ethical decisions about employees. Team members should have a copy of these guidelines so that they can abide by them during the selection process. The following principles from the code apply:

- Hiring shall be based solely on a person's record of accomplishment and ability to carry out the responsibilities.

- In hiring, we shall not participate in any form of discrimination based on race, religion, sex, national origin, handicap, age, or sexual preference. We shall be familiar with laws and regulations that pertain to employment discrimination.

- We shall not hire or recommend for employment any person who is unsuited for a position with respect to competence, qualifications, or character.

Making a Final Decision and Extending an Offer

When you established your interview team, you communicated to the group the type of decision-making model they were engaged in—consultative, collaborative, or delegated. If the understanding is that the team will only make a rank-order recommendation to you (a consultative model) of their preferred candidates, the outcomes of the discussion from tabulating the results of individual rankings on the summary sheets will provide valuable information from which you can make an informed decision. If you are making the decision together with your interview team (a collaborative model) or if you have turned over the responsibility entirely to the team (a delegated model), then the results of the tabulation will constitute the recommendation for an offer.

When the team has completed its deliberations and makes a hire recommendation, it is time to offer employment. Typically, the offer is made in person or by telephone and is followed by written communication detailing the specifics of the offer. Making a formal, written offer allows you to be specific about the position being offered, including all terms and conditions. It should state the salary, benefits, introductory period, and job prerequisites such as rescue breathing training, tuberculosis screening, drug testing, and physical exam. This is a two-way agreement, specifying the conditions to which you both agree. You might also want to identify the things you will do, like provide an orientation program and pre-service training, conduct regular evaluations, and assign a mentor or classroom buddy.

An important part of the employee letter is the description and ultimate implementation of an introductory or alignment period. During this period, which can last from two weeks to perhaps three months, the new employee receives training in job expectations and will have his or her performance evaluated. The alignment period is an adjustment time for the program to get to know the new employee and for the new employee to get to know the program. Hiring mistakes are often revealed during this period, so specifying this time as one of mutual evaluation makes sense. It allows sufficient time for all parties to adjust without allowing a mismatch to continue for too long.

The law considers all employment to be "at-will" unless the parties agree otherwise. "Employment at will" means that either the employer or the employee may terminate the employment relationship at any time, with or without notice, for any reason or for no reason at all. This right of termination has only one constraint—the employer's reason for termination may be bad or irrational, but it may not be illegal. For example, an early childhood center may fire an at-will teacher because the director's brother wants her job or because the staff doesn't like the way the teacher ties her shoes. However, the center may not fire the at-will teacher because she is a certain race, too old, has previously filed a workers' compensation claim, or is a union member.

The parties themselves can defeat the "at-will" relationship by creating a contractual employment relationship. Such a contractual relationship can be explicitly and intentionally created, for example through a written agreement that specifies starting and ending dates of employment and the conditions under which the teacher could be terminated "for cause." Even without a formal written contract, however, employer actions also can defeat the "at-will" relationship. This unintended consequence might occur if an employer established a "good cause" standard for terminations or repeatedly treated the employee as having "permanent" employment. Hence, unless your center has a particular need for a contractual relationship with a new employee, it is critical to emphasize the prospective employee's "at-will" status in the letter offering employment.

The following is an example of an employment letter that includes this clause.

Dear Ms. Brighten:

It is with great pleasure that I offer you the position of infant/toddler teacher at Hickory Woods Child Development Center. We operate a nationally accredited program serving children from six weeks to five years old. Adding talented faculty with your educational background, experience, and expertise allows us to maintain a high standard of quality early care and education for the families we serve.

The starting date for your employment is September 8, 2002. Your employment with Hickory Woods is "at will" and may be terminated by you or the center at any time, for any reason, or without reason and with or without notice. As I discussed in our interview, we hope that all employees make at least a one-year commitment upon hiring in order to maintain continuity of care for enrolled children. In fact, most of our teachers stay with us for much longer periods of time. A compensation sheet is attached detailing your salary and benefits as well as your work schedule.

There are two job prerequisites. The first is that you complete and maintain CPR and first aid certification. We will reimburse you for any fees charged for course participation. The second requirement is that your provide evidence of a TB test and an annual physical stating that you are healthy enough to work with young children.

The first 90 days of your employment are introductory. This is an alignment period for you to get to know the expectations of the center and for us to assess your performance. During this period, you will participate in an orientation program designed to support your success in your teaching role and to provide you with detailed information about your job responsibilities and our expectations for performance. At the end of the introductory period, you will become eligible to accrue vacation and sick leave.

The Code of Ethical Conduct of the National Association for the Education of Young Children and the policies and procedures detailed in the Hickory Woods Personnel Handbook bind all teaching staff. These documents are included in this letter. Also included is your job description.

If you have any questions about your employment, please do not hesitate to call me. To confirm your acceptance of our employment offer, please sign one copy of this letter and return it to me. Keep the extra copy for your records.

Welcome to our center. We look forward to a long and productive relationship.

Sincerely,

The employment letter may also refer to other documents or resources, like your center's personnel policies manual, licensing standards, and accreditation criteria. The employee needs to understand that these are applicable to the job and included by reference in the letter. You may also want to include a reference to the NAEYC's code of ethical conduct or perhaps even include a copy of the brochure.

Since employment laws change frequently, it is a good idea to check with your program's legal counsel or a legal aid organization to determine what laws need to be taken into consideration as you write employment agreements. The reference section in this book includes an online law library of resources that may help you better understand the legal ramifications of your hiring decisions.

A Final Responsibility—The Ethics of Rejection

All applicants who completed applications and/or participated in an interview deserve a response, whether or not they are offered employment. In the continuous recruitment model, the applicants who are not considered for the job have the potential to be kept as a part of the applicant pool. Notifying applicants of the status of their application keeps the door open to reconsideration.

The response can be formal and written or informal and verbal. Formal responses like form letters or e-mail messages may leave the impression that the program was not interested. A telephone call to notify the applicant of his or her status and what will be done to keep the application current may keep the door open on both sides. If you notify an applicant by phone, be sure to document the information that you communicated and any response by the rejected applicant.

If you are able to help the applicant see why he or she was not offered the position—for example, there was a better-qualified applicant, the applicant's salary expectations were out of line with the center's resources, or the applicant's desired work hours were incompatible with the center's needs—the applicant may be able to address these issues and update the application for continued consideration.

At this point many directors feel that the task of recruitment, screening, and selection is over. Although a new teacher has been selected and hired, the process is far from over. Careful, thorough orientation and pre-service training are crucial to ensuring that the teacher you selected will become a successful, long-term employee.

Orienting Right From the Start

When individuals embark on a new job, they are filled with a welter of emotions that range from excitement and anticipation to anxiety and uncertainty. They wonder if they have made the right decision. Will they fit in? Will the job provide the challenge, variety, intellectual stimulation, and recognition that they anticipated it would. Your employee orientation program is designed to keep that excitement alive as well as help individuals discover more about their positions to ensure a good adjustment between expectations and reality. Never again will an employee be as open to suggestions and receptive to your feedback as in those first days and weeks on the job.

Confusion about roles and expectations often begins in the first days (even hours) on the job. Unclear or unexplained expectations are a frequent cause of stress in new job situations. The goal of an employee orientation program is to make expectations clear and confirm that they are understood. If you have never had a formal orientation plan, developing one will help you identify your program's expectations for new employees and think consciously about the specific orientation strategies you can use to communicate your expectations.

Given the importance of the induction phase of employees' socialization into their new jobs, it is unfortunate that the orientation process in many early childhood programs is so haphazard. When it does occur it tends to be too compressed. Perhaps because of the time crunch in which many directors find themselves when filling positions, job orientation often means a cursory review of the center's policies and procedures, a hasty tour of the physical facility, and a stern lecture about critical elements of practice related to licensing and regulations. Many new teachers report that they are thrust into their new jobs with little or no guidance.

When done right, employee orientation programs are the foundation of the center's professional development system. The orientation process sets the stage for the working relationships between new employees, the center's staff, and the children and their families.

Orientation deserves to be comprehensive, systematic, and unrushed. It typically coincides with the introductory period for a new employee, usually between 30 to 90 days. A good orientation program covers the essential technical aspects of the job and center operations, but it focuses also on a larger goal—orienting the new employee to the center's shared values, vision, and mission. In your orientation program you are planting the seeds for growing and keeping staff.

This chapter will help you break down the information that should be covered in an employee orientation program so that by the end of the introductory period your new teacher is fully assimilated into the life of the center—a full-fledged member of your team. You'll learn about different orientation strategies such as using mentors and different ways to provide formal and informal feedback. Finally, you'll learn how to make the orientation process a two-way learning experience where you receive critical feedback about your new teachers that will help you develop individualized professional development plans once their orientation phase is completed.

Designing an Orientation Plan

The first step in orienting right from the start is designing a good orientation plan. Unfortunately, new hires are often needed in the classroom immediately, if not sooner, making it hard to take the time to adequately orient them. Resist the urge to assign new teachers directly to their classrooms if you can. If you can't manage without the teacher taking immediate teaching responsibility, you can still plan a thorough orientation; it just gets a bit harder.

A good place to start is to have a model orientation plan—one that is designed to be put into action every time you hire a new employee. The model plan can serve as a starting point for individualizing orientation for each new employee. A good model plan will incorporate ideas about what the new employee needs to do and learn, when he or she will be introduced to each topic, as well as who is responsible for implementing each part of the orientation.

Build your model orientation plan around your expectations for new employees. Carefully consider the goals you have for the orientation and make a general plan of how you will accomplish your goals. Consider adopting a phased approach as you develop your plan, breaking the orientation content down into manageable amounts of information, varying the training strategies you use across the orientation period, providing adequate two-way communication and feedback, and recognizing and celebrating progress. Let's take a look at how you might design a good orientation plan.

Adopting a Phased Approach

Orienting right from the start takes time. You might want to think about having several phases to your plan. A phased approach helps divide orientation into segments that relate logically to each other and prevents overloading new employees with too much at one time. Think about your orientation plan as having three phases, a welcoming phase, a learning-the-ropes phase, and a skill-building and appraisal phase.

Phase I: Welcome and introduction to your center. First impressions are lasting impressions. How we greet and welcome new teachers during their first few days on the job can set the stage for a productive employer-employee relationship. The first phase of orientation, covering the new employee's first week or two on the job, has two goals. One goal is to ensure that new employees become acquainted with the *essential* requirements of their positions and complete all paperwork required by licensing and sponsoring bodies. The second, and much more important goal, is to help new employees understand your center's culture, values, and vision and their place in it.

Just as good teachers gradually transition young children into new classrooms, think about gradually transitioning new staff into their roles. In a perfect world, the first week of a new teacher's assignments should be preparatory in nature— a gradual introduction to your center and its uniqueness. Few of us live in this perfect world. Nevertheless, this is one time you might consider the costs and benefits of postponing a new teacher's assignment to the classroom to make sure he or she gets off to a good start. Set aside as much time as you can manage where your new teacher is not counted in required ratios. Structure this time to help new employees get acquainted with their colleagues, gain an understanding of the overall structure of your center, and see where they fit into the larger picture. Provide time for them to get to know the teachers, observe in classrooms, cultivate new connections, ask lots of questions, and complete required paperwork.

It is important to start by giving new teachers this view of your total program. You want new teachers to understand how their particular roles dovetail with the overall program. It is natural for teachers to have a micro point of view— focusing their attention on their classrooms and their specific teaching roles. During phase one of your orientation plan, you want to connect new teachers to the larger program, seeing the whole before they begin to address their part.

Some examples of appropriate training activities for this phase of orientation include the following:

- Expanded center tour aimed at familiarizing new teachers with locations in the facility such as bathrooms, staff lounge, storage facilities, and storage for personal belongings

- Brief observation periods in classrooms across the range of ages the center serves aimed at demonstrating your philosophy in action, perhaps supported by written observation guides

- Conversations with human resource staff and completion of new-hire paperwork related to operational topics like payroll, insurance, retirement or other benefits, and leave policies

- Personal introductions to each staff member, perhaps during the expanded tour

- Introduction to *essential* job requirements like first aid and rescue breathing requirements, health and safety requirements like TB testing, annual physicals, location of fire extinguishers, and operating entry systems

- Review of the center's vision statements, philosophy statements, and values statements, followed by discussions with supervisors, peers, or mentors

- Review of work schedule, lunch-break policies, expectations regarding attendance, and professional dress

This list is meant to serve as a springboard for considering the content and format of the first phase of orientation. You can see that the activities listed are typically starting points, not full-fledged, in-depth considerations of the topic. If your orientation plan is sound, you will come back to many of these topics in more depth in later phases, building knowledge and understanding as the new teacher's capacity to retain the information increases.

Phase II: Learning the ropes. During the first phase of orientation, new employees receive an introduction to the critical pieces of information they needed to function in their respective roles and a broad view of the center, its culture, vision, and values. Phase II takes new teachers into their classrooms and into the functions of their new jobs. Time will be spent filling in the gaps and providing additional information and experiences so that new teachers become fully functioning in their jobs. This phase is about really learning the ropes at your center and particularly in the classroom. It is also the time to share more detailed information about the center—its history, background about the sponsoring agency and board of directors, and the short- and long-term centerwide goals as well as details about curriculum, policies, monitoring, licensing, and accreditation.

In this phase the focus usually changes slightly. Up to this point, most of the direction and initiative for training and experiences came from you and your administrative staff. As new teachers get their feet on the ground, they themselves will probably begin to identify what information and experiences might be helpful. Allow some flexibility in this phase to accommodate this natural transition.

The goal of phase two of orientation is to help new teachers understand and explore the educational priorities that shape decision making in your center. The transition from learning information to using it in decision-making situations is a crucial step. When this transition is successful, new teachers will not only understand your program philosophy and how it is implemented, but they will also understand how to use that information to inform their teaching experiences and practice. Making this transition is not guaranteed; supports need to be in place to ensure that it happens.

Compiling easily accessible written resources is a way to help new teachers make the transition to informed decision making and finding their own answers. Written materials may include curriculum plans, examples of completed forms, explanations of specific program policies, and guidelines about how to make decisions in different situations. These materials give new teachers support in making independent decisions, allowing them to look up information before, during, or after a question arises. Build in time for new employees to read all the descriptive literature and information you have given them as well as opportunities to discuss what they have read and what it might mean to them.

Some appropriate training activities a new teacher might engage in during this phase of orientation include the following:

- Review scrapbooks, photo albums, or other evidence of the center's history with a co-worker who has been employed at the center for several years

- Further exploration of organizational charts, reporting responsibilities, grievance procedures, expectations for confidentiality, promotion and tenure policies, professional ethics, risk management procedures, and child abuse reporting requirements

- An introduction to curriculum philosophy, goals, planning approaches, sources of curriculum ideas, policies and procedures for field trips and outdoor playground activities

- Review the center's approach to child guidance, child assessment, parent relationships and participation

- Create a mini bio-board for display outside the new teachers' classroom as an introduction to parents

- Observation in other classrooms focusing on child guidance strategies, hand-washing procedures, norms for greeting children, classroom setup, lunch and nap time routines, use of communication logs

- Review the center's annual calendar to understand the yearly schedule, holidays, how curriculum varies over the year, and seasonal special events planned by the center

- Practice emergency procedures and drills

- Preliminary competency self-evaluation using the center's evaluation instruments

- Evaluate progress in orientation

Again, this list is not all-inclusive but can serve as a starting place for identifying content and training strategies for this phase.

Another way to help new teachers during this second phase of the orientation process is to form mentor relationships with other teachers. Using mentors continues the early connections that were formed as new teachers got to know the other personnel at the center. Mentors can play many roles and support ongoing orientation for new teachers. We'll talk more about mentoring a little later.

Don't forget to plan frequent opportunities for feedback and evaluation into your orientation plan. A thorough discussion of evaluation and feedback strategies is included later in this chapter and can be used to make sure your plan has many chances for new teachers to hear about how they are doing and to give new teachers chances to ask for more help in areas that are challenging or troubling them.

Phase III: Skill building and final appraisal of fit. Orientation now shifts to helping new teachers function optimally in their positions. Because new teachers bring different knowledge, skills, and abilities to the job, this part of the orientation process needs to be individualized. For example, an experienced new teacher may be very knowledgeable about assessment strategies for children. If so, she just needs to know about and understand the particular approach used in your program and have opportunities to practice using the forms and procedures. In this situation, you can individualize the orientation to provide an overview for the experienced teacher, pairing her up with her mentor to review and practice assessment process. If, on the other hand, the new teacher is inexperienced with assessment, she will need more support in understanding the approach used in your program and how to put it to use. In this situation, you will need to start at the beginning, helping the inexperienced teacher see how assessment is integrated into the program before moving on to how to do it.

Some examples of appropriate training activities for this phase of orientation include the following:

- Viewing videotapes, audiotapes, computer programs, or published resources on specific topics of importance to the center's philosophy

- Conversations with a mentor to discuss observations, issues, concerns, or questions that have come up during orientation

- Demonstration teaching observed by a mentor to note strengths and suggest improvement strategies

- Targeted observation of teachers with high levels of skill in particular content or process areas

- Observation of a parent/teacher conference or parent meeting

- Peer evaluation on a limited number of specific skills in teaching

- Attendance at professional development meetings with a colleague

- Reading training modules and completing post-test evaluation of knowledge, skills, or understanding

- Discussion of written materials with a small group of other new teachers

You can see that these training experiences are more complex, building on the experiences of the previous stages to get new teachers really ready to proceed on their own in the classroom. When orientation continues until new employees reach this level of understanding and sophistication about the center and its program, the chances of ultimate success increase dramatically.

Final appraisal of fit is a crucial part of this phase. If your orientation plan had many opportunities to assess new hires' progress and determine how they fit into your center, you will have a good sense of the how the employee is adapting to the culture of your center and meeting the expectations for performance as well as an idea about those areas that may still require work.

One thing worse than training people and losing them is not training them and keeping them.

Zig Ziglar

Sample Orientation Plan

Phase I	Responsible Person
Getting acquainted; expanded tour—use floor plan; locate and label locker; staff introductions; meet mentor; distribution of staff manual, operating procedures manual, accreditation standards, licensing, standards, etc.	Director
Historical overview, vision, values, and mission statements; discussion with director about center's priorities and goals.	Director
Organizational overview, paperwork completion; introduction to job-related requirements like rescue breathing, annual physical, drug testing, etc.	Administrative assistant
Thirty-minute observation periods, one classroom of each age level, using observation worksheet; discussion with human resources staff.	Director, human resources staff
Introduction to health and safety, emergency procedures, sanitation, and children's health records.	Assistant director
Evaluation of progress/check in with new hire	Director

Phase II	Responsible Person
Review historical documents, photo albums, and talk about center's history.	Director
Discussion about reporting responsibilities, particularly how to get help with problems.	Director
Introduction to curriculum approach and overview of positive guidance techniques; overview of other guiding philosophies or viewpoints.	Curriculum coordinator
Create introduction display board.	New hire
Focused observation in same-age classrooms using observation worksheets; discussion with curriculum coordinator.	Curriculum coordinator
Emergency drill observation; emergency procedure review; classroom drill practice.	Emergency drill coordinator
Review annual calendar.	Administrative assistant
Preliminary self-evaluation; complete Staff Orientation Assessment; discussion with director.	New hire, director
Evaluation of progress with new hire.	Director

Sample Orientation Plan (cont'd)	

Phase III	Responsible Person
View videotapes with mentor.	Mentor
Written observation of classroom; discuss with mentor.	Mentor
Demonstration teaching as needed.	Mentor, director, teachers
Observe targeted teachers with high levels of competence in new hire's areas for improvement; follow-up discussion with observed teacher.	New hire, targeted teachers
Complete self-paced training modules; complete outcome evaluation for each module.	Mentor, administrative staff
Written material review; small group discussion.	New hire, mentor, director
Attend parent meeting; observe parent/teacher conference conducted by mentor.	Mentor
Peer evaluation by mentor.	Mentor
Assessment of progress; develop professional development plan.	Mentor, director

Breaking Training Content into Segments

Teachers have many job functions. They are responsible for the early care and education of children, planning curriculum, working with parents, organizing the environment, making toys and teaching materials, maintaining health and safety guidelines, preventing emergencies, communicating with other teachers, assessing children's development, and so on. New staff, even if they are experienced, should not be expected to learn about or handle all of these functions at once. A good orientation plan identifies which of these job functions will be targeted first, second, and so on, until you and your new teachers have a chance to examine their skill level in particular job functions, learn new information or practice new skills, and assess what additional support is needed to continue to grow professionally.

For most new teachers, it is helpful to break orientation competencies (both content and skills) into manageable segments—small enough units that the information can be acquired, understood, and put into practice. There are many ways to organize this part of your orientation. Using a recognized structure like the Child Development Associate (CDA) functional areas developed by the Council for Early Childhood Professional Recognition or the accreditation criteria of the NAEYC Academy for Early Childhood Program Accreditation can serve as framework for breaking down competency expectations into manageable segments. Some training curricula like *Innovations: The Comprehensive Infant/Toddler Curriculum* or *The Creative Curriculum* also have trainer's guides that can be used to structure content during this orientation phase.

To illustrate this idea of breaking training down into manageable segments, let's look at how a curriculum might be introduced using this approach. Curriculum is a collection of broad concepts that focus on the particular way your center teaches children. It covers, for example, observations of children, room arrangement, toys, supplies and equipment, schedule, child guidance, and activities and experiences in all areas of development, parent communication, and family involvement.

Obviously, all of these areas need to be part of every teacher's knowledge base, experience, skills, and abilities. Yet, if you approach curriculum from this broad point of view, you will probably overwhelm inexperienced teachers and insult experienced teachers. The result is that you will not be able to appropriately identify the range of a new teacher's strengths and the areas in need of improvement. Instead, plan to break down your content about different curriculum areas across the three phases of your orientation, placing segments or topics where they logically fall. The chart on page 93 illustrates the idea of integrating phases and manageable training segments across the entire orientation period, resulting in a new teacher who is thoroughly oriented to your center's view of curriculum by the end of their introductory period.

Teachers introduced to your center's curriculum in this fashion will have a relatively complete understanding of how curriculum is planned, implemented, and evaluated by the end of their formal orientation.

Varying Training Strategies During Orientation

To the extent possible, baseline training provided during the three phases of orientation should take a hands-on approach—helping new employees apply what they learn on their jobs through active, participatory, experiential learning strategies. Experiential training considers adult-learning styles, uses effective learning strategies, includes different types of individual intelligences, and presents information in a variety of ways. After you develop the framework and

Breaking Down the Training Content During Orientation

Curriculum area	Phase I	Phase II	Phase III
Health and safety	X Introduction	X Procedures and drills	X Universal precautions and sanitation
Observation of children			X
Room arrangement, toys, and supplies	X		
Daily schedule		X	
Child guidance and discipline	X General policy	X Positive guidance	X Collaborating with parents
Social development			X
Emotional development	X		X
Cognitive development			X
Physical development and outdoor play		X	
Parent communication, participation, and involvement	X Policy and openness	X Involving parents	X Parent/teacher conferences

plan for your orientation, make sure you vary the training strategies you use across the plan. It may also be helpful to develop some support tools like observation forms, note-taking worksheets, or other tools for bringing the activities and experiences of orientation to life.

Using Mentors

As you develop your orientation plan, consider using mentors to facilitate the process. Creating mentor/protégé relationships allows some of the orientation to take place with peers. When mentoring works, everyone wins. What could be better than having an experienced teacher take a personal interest in a new teacher's success? The benefits of mentoring go beyond the immediate acquisition of knowledge and skills for the new teacher.

Mentoring helps both the new teacher and the experienced teacher grow. In a good mentor/protégé relationship, the protégé feels supported in gaining useful knowledge and skills, while the mentor's teaching talents are validated and acknowledged. Mentoring, however, must be voluntary. Without willingness, it is easy for the mentor to let the job slip—defeating the purpose of mentoring for both mentor and protégé.

Logistically, mentors need opportunities to observe their protégés at work. Observation is most naturally facilitated when mentors and protégés work in close proximity, share outdoor space at regular periods, or have overlapping planning time. Mentors and protégés need to be able to communicate freely so that situations, problems, and questions can be addressed as they occur. Substitute coverage may be necessary during the orientation phase to provide the released time for mentors to meet with new employees.

As in any teaching situation, a structure should be in place to support mentor relationships. Structures that evolve naturally from the mentoring process are easiest to use. Shared planning times, observations of each other at work in the classroom, attendance at training sessions, informal discussions to reflect on teaching practices, and viewing child development videos together are just some of the many orientation training activities that mentors and protégés can experience together. Add these to your orientation plan.

Providing Feedback as an Integral Strategy

While feedback is important in the supervisory and performance appraisal process for all employees, it is particularly crucial during the orientation of new employees. Often new employees are too unfamiliar with their surroundings and the personalities of those with whom they work to pick up the subtle cues about how they are doing. For this reason, frequent and systematic feedback for new employees is imperative. Even high-performing teachers are hungry for feedback when they first begin new jobs.

Set up a system of formal and informal opportunities to provide feedback to new employees, giving them ample information about how they are progressing. Pay attention to the type, quantity, quality, and frequency of your feedback. Early in a new teacher's tenure, give more emphasis to positive feedback than to constructive feedback, increasing constructive feedback as your relationship with the new teacher grows. Starting with the positive makes sense. New teachers are often more self-critical than their supervisors. Pointing out the skills that are already in place builds a sense of confidence in new teachers, supporting their feelings of competence.

Feedback should come from many sources in order to give your new employees different perspectives of how they are doing. Share the responsibility for providing informal feedback with your entire administrative team. Help them see that they all have a role in coaching, motivating, and training new employees.

Varying the types of feedback. Vary your techniques for providing feedback. This will help communicate the message in different ways. Feedback such as written evaluations, observation, face-to-face meetings, personal notes offering encouragement, and casual comments in the hallway during lulls in the day will help satisfy a new teacher's hunger for direction and support. The table on page 96 summarizes the many formal and informal ways you can provide feedback.

Don't forget self-evaluation. You might ask new teachers to keep a journal during orientation reflecting on the joys, frustrations, and challenges of beginning a new job. Begin every formal feedback checkpoint by asking the new teacher to share his or her feelings and insights with you. This reinforces your expectation that good teachers are reflective practitioners.

A formal evaluation of strengths and areas in need of improvement should take place at the end of the first 30 days and again at the end of your 90-day introductory period. Some directors even schedule a third formal assessment at the 60-day marker. This is particularly advisable for inexperienced staff where the orientation plan provides baseline training and skill building. Taking time to complete a formal performance assessment is just as important for highly skilled teachers who are adapting quickly to the job and the center. Formal evaluation ensures that everyone is on the same page and sees performance the same way.

Formal checkpoints of progress are particularly important if the new teacher is having difficulty in adjusting to or performing the job. It is unfair for teachers to find out at the end of their introductory period that they are failing. By then it's too late. Teachers who are struggling in their new jobs should hear about it at many points during the orientation period, not when the opportunity to change the outcome is lost.

Making feedback reciprocal. In addition to providing frequent feedback to new personnel, it is also important to get feedback from new employees about how they feel the orientation process is proceeding. Tapping into employees' perceptions about the orientation process helps create the foundation of a relationship based on mutual trust and respect. It also circumvents potential problems so they don't have a chance to grow into full-blown job grievances. In addition, practice in giving feedback to supervisors and mentors during the orientation phase of employment will ensure that the employees know how to get information to you about how they are doing after the orientation ends.

Types of Feedback

	Oral	Written
Formal	Face-to-face conferences with supervisors and mentors	Face-to-face conferences with supervisors and mentors
	Peer evaluations by colleagues or mentors	Peer evaluation by colleagues or mentors
	Check-in points (either time sequenced or event sequenced)	Individual, classroom, or centerwide evaluations
	Classroom observation	Classroom observation
	Reflection about experiences	Reflection about experiences
	Introduction and recognition at staff meetings	Notes from parents, mentors, colleagues, and supervisors.
	Sharing comments or compliments from parents, mentors, colleagues, and others	Checklists
		Videotape reviews
		Questionnaires
Informal	Verbal comments that emerge from spontaneous, informal observations	Bulletin board messages and postings
	Reporting positive comments from parents or peers	Bathroom or staff-room message boards
	Telephone calls	Keep-in-touch notebooks
	Self-evaluation of experiences	Self-evaluation of experiences

Adapted from Albrecht, K. (1990). Helping teachers grow: Strategies for diversifying evaluation and feedback. Child Care Information Exchange, 74, 34-36. Reprinted with permission.

Appendix I provides an orientation assessment form you can use with your new staff. Ideally, it should be given to new staff four to six weeks after they have begun working at your program. It is recommended that the employee have the opportunity to take the assessment home and complete it without the distractions of the classroom.

Because the responses on this assessment tool are open ended, they will vary from individual to individual. The results will alert you to potential misunderstandings about the scope and nature of the position assumed. The results can also prove helpful in modifying orientation practices for new staff in the future.

Completing the Orientation Phase of Employment

Conclude the initial alignment or introductory period for your new employees by formally recognizing that they have completed their orientation program. Share their success with colleagues, mentors, and parents.

At this point, complete a written training plan for the next three to six months that commits to continuing professional development of the teacher and negotiates how it will be implemented and evaluated. By planning ongoing training, building in evaluation and feedback opportunities, and committing to continuing growth in teaching skills, you cement the relationship between the teacher and the school. You can put these important milestones on your administrative calendar to ensure that each is reached and recognized.

No question about it—a phased orientation with many built-in opportunities to assess employee performance early in the relationship is an effective strategy for promoting successful retention among staff. New teachers who get this kind of support and feedback during the early months of their teaching experiences are far more likely to develop into autonomous, capable teachers and to feel committed to your center as a viable place for long-term employment and professional development.

IT FITS! IT FITS!

CHAPTER 7

A Final Word

One usually hears a collective sigh from administrative staff when the recruitment, selection, and orientation process for new staff is complete. Directors feel like they can finally get back to doing their *real* job—the one placed on hold as the hiring process played out. In reality, the circle is just completed and begins again. This is the vital and real work of being an early childhood administrator. It is the essence of effective leadership.

We started the journey toward finding new employees with the right fit by looking at all the challenges directors face when they survey the landscape of early care and education. Infrastructure issues that plague our profession were discussed, with the focus on showing that some issues are larger than your day-to-day experiences in the world of program operation. Then a new model was proposed for the recruitment phase of the process of finding new staff. The new recruitment model included the important leadership idea of being prepared for change by creating and implementing a continuous recruitment plan designed to keep a steady flow of applicants headed toward your door.

In our discussion about implementing a continuous recruitment plan, we stressed that a great deal of effort must go into assessing the fit of the applicants with the available job and the center. It requires the entire faculty and staff to focus their attention on identifying unique features of the center to help evaluate fit during interviews. Careful screening follows this step as you look critically at applicants who submit their credentials for consideration. Devising good questions to ask, planning the interviews, and strategizing about ways to identify goodness of fit between applicants and the center as part of the process. The interview team then conducts the interviews and gathers data you need to make a decision about the applicant with the best fit for the vacant position.

Finally, we embraced the idea that new teachers deserve a comprehensive and thorough introduction to their new job. This is accomplished by designing and implementing a three-phase orientation to induct the new hires into the culture, climate, and competencies of the center. The introductory period is critical for testing how appropriate your hiring decisions were. It is the time to see the candidate in action. Careful monitoring and support during the orientation phase is the only way to ensure that the candidate is indeed the right fit for the position.

Continuous recruitment and thorough screening, interviewing, selecting, and orienting of new staff is essential for program success. How will you know if your efforts at continuous recruitment are working? When you are able to respond to the resignation of an employee without panic and anxiety, and when it is relatively easy to generate a pool of applicants who meet or exceed the requirements of the vacant position, continuous recruitment is working for you.

After each position is filled, formally evaluate the effectiveness of your plan. Begin by interviewing new hires to discover why they responded to your job advertisement or recruitment strategy. Ask them how they learned about your center, what they found attractive in your ad, how they perceived the interviewing process, and why they accepted the job offer. Tracking this data over time will help you zero in on the recruitment strategies that work best, identify seasonal differences in responses, and give you more ideas about how to successfully spend your recruitment, screening, selection, interviewing, and orientation time.

As you consider the design of your plan, you will want to add new ideas and rework or omit ones that don't. Your plan should be dynamic—changing over time until you refine and perfect it.

Ultimately the measure of success in recruiting will be the spirit of collegiality that prevails among staff and the standards of performance that guide professional practice at your center. If interview strategies have successfully identified candidates with a good fit for your center, and if your employee orientation program helps raise the competence bar, then you should begin to see a decrease in turnover and an increase in shared commitment to high-quality early care and education programming. The feeling that results is one of confidence in your ability to find teachers who have the right fit for your program—and that feels pretty good!

For Further Reading

Albrecht, K. (1990, August). Helping teachers grow: Strategies for diversifying performance evaluation and feedback. *Child Care Information Exchange*, 74, 34-36.

Albrecht, K., Dziadul, L., Gwinn, C., & Harrington, B. (2001). The good, the bad, and the wonderful: Keeping children and teachers together (Part 2), *Child Care Information Exchange*, 137, 90-93.

Alvarado, C. (2002, January/February). Voices in search of cultural continuity in communities. *Child Care Information Exchange*, 143, 42-44.

Balfour, D.L., & Neff, D.M. (1993). Predicting and managing turnover in human services agencies: A case study of an organization in crisis. *Public Personnel Management*, 22(3), 473-86.

Bloom, P.J. (2002). *Making the most of meetings: A practical guide*. Lake Forest, IL: New Horizons.

Bloom, P.J. (2000). *Circle of influence: Implementing shared decision making and participative management*. Lake Forest, IL: New Horizons.

Bloom, P.J., Sheerer, M., & Britz, J. (1991). *Blueprint for action: Achieving center-based change through staff development*. Lake Forest, IL: New Horizons.

Bredekamp, S., & Copple, C. (Eds.). (1997). *Developmentally appropriate practice in early childhood programs*. Revised edition. Washington, DC: National Association for the Education of Young Children.

Carter, M. (2001, March/April). What should we be emphasizing? *Child Care Information Exchange*, 138, 82-85.

Carter, M., & Curtis, D. (1994). *Training teachers: A harvest of theory and practice*. St. Paul, MN: Redleaf.

Cartwright, S. (1999). What makes good early childhood teachers? *Young Children*, 54(4), 4-7.

Center for the Child Care Workforce. (2001). *Current data on child care salaries and benefits in the United States*. Washington, DC: Author.

Children's Defense Fund. (2001). *The state of America's children: 2001 yearbook*. Washington, DC: Author.

Council for Early Childhood Professional Recognition. (1993). *CDA competency standards and assessment system*. Washington, DC: Author.

Decker, C., & Decker, J. (2001). *Planning and administering early childhood programs.* Columbus, OH: Merrill Prentice Hall.

Dodge, D. T., Yandian, S. E., & Bloomer, D. (1998). *The trainer's guide to The Creative Curriculum for Infants and Toddlers.* Washington, DC: Teaching Strategies.

Epstein, A. S. (2002, January/February). Early childhood professions: Current status and projected needs. *Child Care Information Exchange,* 143, 45-48.

Feeney, S., & Freeman, N.K. (1999). *Ethics and the early childhood educator.* Washington, DC: National Association for the Education of Young Children.

Glick, P., Scott, F., & Eggbeer, L. (2000). Selecting staff for infant/family programs: Issues and strategies. *Zero to Three,* 21(2), 44-50.

Hamrick, J. (2000, July/August). Reduce staff turnover through effective interviewing. *Child Care Information Exchange,* 134, 26-28.

Heng, A.C. (2001, September/October). Hiring the right person. *Child Care Information Exchange,* 141, 10-12.

Meservey, L. (1993, July/August). Implications of the Americans with Disabilities Act. *Child Care Information Exchange,* 92, 81-83.

Miller, L., & Albrecht, K. (2001). *The comprehensive infant & toddler curriculum: Trainer's guide.* Beltsville, MD: Gryphon House.

Murray, K. (1986, March). Points to consider in providing references. *Child Care Information Exchange,* 25-26.

National Association for the Education of Young Children. (1998). *Guidelines for accreditation.* Washington, DC: Author.

Neugebauer, B., & Neugebauer R. (Eds.). (1998). *The art of leadership: Managing early childhood organizations.* Redmond, WA: Exchange Press.

Perreault, J., & Neugebauer, R. (1998). Developing your employee handbook: Job descriptions. In B. Neugebauer & R. Neugebauer (Eds.), *The art of leadership: Managing early childhood organizations* (pp. 174-177). Redmond, WA: Exchange Press.

Sheerer, M., & Bloom, P.J. (1990). The ongoing challenge: Attracting and retaining quality staff. *Child Care Information Exchange,* 72, 11-16.

Sciarra, D. J., & Dorsey, A. G. (2002). *Leaders and supervisors in child care programs.* Albany, NY: Delmar.

Shiller, P., & Dyke, P.C. (2001). *A practical guide to quality child care*. Beltsville, MD: Gryphon House.

U.S. Bureau of Labor Statistics. (2001). *Survey output*. Washington, DC: Author.

Whitebook, M., & Bellm, D. (1999). *Taking on turnover: An action guide for child care center teachers and directors*. Washington, DC: Center for the Child Care Workforce.

Whitebook, M., Phillips, D., & Howes, C. (1993). *National Child Care Staffing Study revisited: Four years in the life of center-based child care*. Oakland, CA: Child Care Employee Project.

Zeece, P.D. (1997, July/August). Investing in hire education. *Child Care Information Exchange*, 116, 12-18.

For written information about federal and state employment law, contact the American Chamber of Commerce Publishers (www.hrcomply.com) to purchase a comprehensive guide for your state.

Online Law Library

Looking for information about a specific issue related to federal employment law? Check out these Websites for helpful online resources.

The Family and Medical Leave Act (FMLA) provides eligible employees with up to 12 weeks of unpaid, job-protected leave per year for certain family- and health-related reasons. For general information about employee eligibility, benefits during leave, returning to work after leave, and record-keeping requirements, see www.elaws.dol.gov/fmla/wren/sl.htm

The Health Insurance Portability and Accountability Act (HIPAA) provides rights and protections for participants in group health plans when they change or lose their jobs. For general information about HIPAA, see www.askpwba.dol.gov/faq-compliance-hipaa.html

Unemployment Insurance (UI) is a state-federal partnership financed by two different employer taxes. At the state level, agencies collect quarterly employer contributions (taxes) to pay unemployment benefits to eligible, unemployed workers. For contribution rate determinations, quarterly filing requirements, and "fast facts" for Illinois* employers, click on www.ides.state.il.us/employer/uitax/index.htm

The Consolidated Omnibus Budget Reconciliation Act (COBRA) provides temporary continuation of health coverage to terminated workers at group rates offered through employers. For information about employer requirements, benefit entitlements, and premium payments, see www.askpwba.dol.gov/fap-compliance-cobra.html

The Employee Retirement Income Security Act (ERISA) is a federal law that governs pension plans, profit-sharing stock bonuses, and most "welfare benefit plans," such as health and life insurance. ERISA sets uniform minimum standards to ensure that such plans are established and maintained in a fair and financially sound manner. For more details, link to www.dol.gov/asp/programs/handbook/erisa

The **Child Labor** provisions of the **Fair Labor Standards Act** are designed to protect children under 18 years from work conditions that are detrimental to their health and well-being. For information about age restrictions, work hours, meal and rest period provisions, and wage standards, see www.dol.gov/dol/topic/youthlabor/index.htm

Minimum wage and overtime pay laws are included in the Fair Labor Standards Act (FLSA). For information about employee classification and wage standards that applies to both the employer and employee, see www.dol.gov/dol/topics/wages/minimumwage.htm

Equal Employment Opportunity Laws are the federal laws that prohibit job discrimination. Among them are Title VII of the Civil Rights Act of 1964, the Equal Pay Act of 1963 (EPA), the Age Discrimination in Employment Act of 1967 (ADEA), and the Americans with Disabilities Act of 1990 (ADA). For more information, see www.eeoc.gov

IRS Rules for Hiring include information related to Employer Identification Numbers (EIN), wage reporting, employment eligibility determination, and record-keeping requirements. All necessary publications and forms can be downloaded from www.irs.ustreas.gov/business/index.html

Federal Employment taxes exist in four forms: Federal income tax, Social Security tax, Medicare tax, and Federal unemployment (FUTA) tax. For more information about withholding requirements, payment schedules, and other compliance guidelines, see www.ustreas.gov/sitemap/index.html

The Child Care Law Center provides a wide range of resources relating to early childhood legal issues. Contact www.childcarelaw.org

The Immigration Reform and Control Act of 1986 requires employers to verify that all employees are legally authorized to work in the United States. Contact the INS to receive the employment forms you need and learn about immigration issues. The INS can be reached at www.ins.usdoj.gov/graphics/index.htm

* *Consult the employment and labor agencies in your state for additional information relating to state-specific labor laws. Most state agencies states maintain Websites with useful information and forms.*

Appendices

My Networking Contacts

Local business groups	Contact person	Contact information

Directors support groups	Contact person	Contact information

Professional associations	Contact person	Contact information

Colleges and universities	Contact person	Contact information

Resource and referral agencies	Contact person	Contact information

Other community organizations	Contact person	Contact information

Professional Activities Questionnaire

Rationale:
Professional involvement of teachers and administrators promotes growth and change, knowledge-based skill, reference-group orientation, and achievement of goals. Individuals with a strong professional orientation also tend to have a stronger commitment to the center and more enthusiasm about their work. This tool assesses the type and variety of activities an individual engages in that promote professionalism.

Directions:
The kind of information elicited on this questionnaire provides important background data on a prospective candidate for employment at your center. Individuals should be instructed to answer the 13 questions as completely as possible.

Scoring:
The scores on this instrument range from a low of 0 to a high of 20. The following may be used as a guide for scoring the 13 questions included on this assessment tool:

1. just a job = 0, a career = 1

2. no = 0, yes = 1

3. no = 0, yes = 1

4. 0 to 5 hrs = 0, 6 to 10 hrs = 1, more than 10 hrs = 2

5. give 1 point for each different organization noted up to 2 points (note that NAEYC and its affiliates ILAEYC, CAEYC, HAEYC, etc. are considered only one organization)

6. give 1 point for each educational magazine or journal noted, up to 2 points

7. none = 0, 1-3 = 1, 4 or more = 2

8. none = 0, 1 = 1, 2 or more = 2

9. none = 0, 1-3 = 1, 4 or more = 2

10. none = 0, 1 = 1, 2 or more = 2

11. 1 point if title and publisher are noted

12. no = 0, yes = 1

13. no = 0, yes = 1

From Bloom, P. J., Sheerer, M., & Britz, J. (1991). Blueprint for action: Achieving center-based change through staff development. Lake Forest, IL: New Horizons. (Assessment Tool #20, pp 242-243). Reprinted with permission.

Professional Activities

1. Do you consider your work _____ just a job or _____ a career?

2. Did you enroll in any college courses for credit last year?   no _____   yes _____

3. Are you currently working toward a degree or credential?   no _____   yes _____

4. On the average, how many hours per week do you spend over and above what you are paid for in activities related to early childhood? _____ hours

5. What professional organizations do you currently pay dues to?

   _____   _____

6. What professional journals and/or magazines do you currently subscribe to?

   _____   _____

7. How many professional books did you read last year?

   _____ none   _____ 1 to 3   _____ 4 or more

8. How many advocacy letters to elected representatives or to the editor of your local newspaper have you written during the past year?

   _____ none   _____ 1   _____ 2 or more

9. How many professional conferences/workshops did you attend last year?

   _____ none   _____ 1 to 3   _____ 4 or more

10. How many workshops or lectures did you present to professional groups during the past year (not counting your own staff)?

    _____ none   _____ 1   _____ 2 or more

11. Have you published any articles or books on early childhood education?

    Title/publisher _____

12. Do you expect to be working in the field of early childhood three years from now?

    _____ no   _____ yes   If no, why? _____

13. If you could do it all over again, would you choose a career in early childhood education?

    _____ no   _____ yes   Why? _____

From Bloom, P. J., Sheerer, M., & Britz., J. (1991). Blueprint for action: Achieving center-based change through staff development. Lake Forest, IL: New Horizons. (Assessment Tool #20, pp 242-243). Reprinted with permission.

APPENDIX C

Beliefs and Values Questionnaire

Rationale:
Teachers' attitudes and beliefs about children provide the foundation for their philosophy of teaching. Because beliefs are grounded in one's values, they have a strong impact on shaping behavior. Teachers' values also govern how they react when confronted with the ethical dilemmas that occur from time to time. The director's role is to ensure that the beliefs and values of individual teachers are consonant with the shared beliefs and stated philosophy of the center.

This assessment asks teachers to reflect on their attitudes and beliefs about children, parents, and their own teaching role in the classroom. The information gleaned from this self-assessment will help you to better understand the values and beliefs that drive the teaching practices of a particular teacher candidate.

Directions:
Explain to the candidate that there are no right or wrong answers in completing this assessment. The purpose is to gather information regarding their beliefs and values about working with young children. To follow up during the interview you may want to ask the candidate how his or her responses to some of the questions on this questionnaire have changed over time.

From Bloom, P. J., Sheerer, M., & Britz., J. (1991). Blueprint for action: Achieving center-based change through staff development. Lake Forest, IL: New Horizons. (Assessment Tool #18, pp 232-233). Reprinted with permission.

Beliefs and Values

Values are enduring beliefs—ideas that we cherish and regard highly. Values influence the decisions we make and the course of action we follow. Some values we prize more deeply than others; they become standards by which we live. The purpose of this assessment is to provide an opportunity for you to share the values and beliefs that guide your teaching practices.

PART I. Complete the following sentences.

1. I think children are generally _____

2. When children are unhappy, it's usually because _____

3. I get angry when children _____

4. The most important thing a teacher can do is _____

5. Children should not _____

6. All children are _____

7. I wish parents would _____

8. When parents _____ I feel _____

PART II. Circle the five traits and characteristics you would like children to be or have as a result of their preschool experience with you.

adventurous	appreciates beauty	determined
affectionate	inquisitive	energetic
polite	respectful	friendly
altruistic	self-starter	obedient
caring	sense of humor	spontaneous
honest	industrious	persistent
assertive	creative	proud
confident	independent thinker	risk-taker
cheerful	desire to excel	open-minded

From Bloom, P. J., Sheerer, M., & Britz., J. (1991). *Blueprint for action: Achieving center-based change through staff development*. Lake Forest, IL: New Horizons. (Assessment Tool #18, pp 232-233). Reprinted with permission.

Identifying and Writing Fit Criteria

Think about your ideal job applicant with respect to the following job and center characteristics. Write one or two criteria that you might use to determine which applicants would be a good fit.

Criteria relating to your program philosophy:

_____

_____

Criteria about expectations for co-worker relations:

_____

_____

Criteria about expectations for parent relations:

_____

_____

Criteria relating to the fit with your leadership and management style:

_____

_____

Criteria relating to expectations for communication and conflict resolution:

_____

_____

Criteria relating to the physical environment and instructional resources:

_____

_____

Criteria for filling gaps in the staff's collective expertise:

_____

_____

Criteria relating to level of general education, early childhood training, and experience:

_____

_____

Criteria relating to specialized knowledge, skills, and dispositions desired for the job:

_____

_____

Criteria about expectations for ongoing professional development:

_____

_____

Criteria for expectations for specific job responsibilities:

_____

_____

Criteria relating to salary and benefits:

_____

_____

Criteria about expectations for promotion and increases in compensation:

_____

_____

Criteria relating to work style:

_____

_____

Other criteria:

_____

_____

_____

_____

_____

_____

_____

_____

Application for Employment

<table>
<tr><td rowspan="6">P E R S O N A L</td><td>Last name   First   Middle or Maiden</td><td>Date</td></tr>
<tr><td>Street address</td><td>Social Security No.</td></tr>
<tr><td>City, state, zip</td><td>E-mail address</td></tr>
<tr><td>Home phone (   )   Business phone (   )</td><td>Pay expected</td></tr>
<tr><td>Position desired</td><td>Date available to begin work?</td></tr>
<tr><td colspan="2">Are you legally eligible for employment in the United States? ❑ yes   ❑ no</td></tr>
</table>

	SCHOOL	NAME AND ADDRESS OF SCHOOL	COURSE OF STUDY	NO. OF YEARS COMPLETED	DIPLOMA OR DEGREE
E D U C A T I O N	High				
	College				
	Other (Specify)				

MEMBERSHIP IN PROFESSIONAL OR COMMUNITY ORGANIZATIONS
(You may omit those that disclose your race, religious creed, color, national origin, ancestry, sex, age, or any other status protected by applicable law)

PROFESSIONAL ACHIEVEMENTS, HONORS, AND AWARDS

EMPLOYMENT RECORD

Please list present and past employment (full time and part time), beginning with most recent.

Organization	Telephone ( )
Street address City State Zip	Employed (give month and year) From To
Name of supervisor	Salary
Job Title	Reason for leaving

Organization	Telephone ( )
Street address City State Zip	Employed (give month and year) From To
Name of supervisor	Salary
Job Title	Reason for leaving

Organization	Telephone ( )
Street address City State Zip	Employed (give month and year) From To
Name of supervisor	Salary
Job Title	Reason for leaving

Organization	Telephone ( )
Street address City State Zip	Employed (give month and year) From To
Name of supervisor	Salary
Job Title	Reason for leaving

List names, addresses, and contact information of three references that are not family members.

1. _____   phone: _____
   _____

2. _____   phone: _____
   _____

3. _____   phone: _____
   _____

I give permission to [NAME OF CENTER] to contact these references. _____
                                                                          (Signature)

Preliminary Screening Form

Name of applicant _____ Date _____

Application	Yes	No
Complete?		
Information still needed:		

Educational requirements	Yes	No
General education requirements met?		
Specialized education requirements met?		
Desired education requirements met?		
Strengths: Questions:		

Experience requirements	Yes	No
Experience requirements met?		
Desirable experience requirements met?		
Strengths: Questions:		

Job history	Yes	No
Job history complete?		
Strengths: Questions:		

Salary history	Yes	No
Salary history complete?		
Questions:		

References	Yes	No
References contact information complete?		

Initial reference check	Yes	No
Recommended for rehire?		
Application information confirmed?		
Issues raised:		

Preliminary recommendation:

❑ Proceed with interview   ❑ Do not proceed with interview

Form completed by: _____

Interview Summary

Applicant _____ Date _____

Position _____ Interviewer _____

Category	Areas considered
Previous work experience *(note comments)* weak 1 2 3 4 5 strong	Relevance of experience Level of responsibility Flexibility exhibited Level of productivity Interpersonal relations Leadership exhibited Notable achievements
General and specialized education weak 1 2 3 4 5 strong	Relevance of education Intellectual abilities Breadth and depth of study Notable academic achievements Specialized expertise
Personal characteristics unfavorable 1 2 3 4 5 favorable	General appearance Interpersonal interactions Oral communication skills Punctuality Level of enthusiasm and vitality Maturity and judgment exhibited Diversity of interests
Fit with the job poor 1 2 3 4 5 excellent	Specialized knowledge needed Skills and behaviors needed Dispositions needed General work style Physical demands
Fit with the center poor 1 2 3 4 5 excellent	Values, beliefs, philosophy Attitudes about parent relations Leadership potential Adds new expertise to staff Adds cultural diversity

Summary of strengths (+)

Summary of weaknesses (-)

Recommendation (note reasons)

1. In favor of hiring (stress value and assets)

2. Against hiring (note risks or liabilities)

OVERALL RATING   unfavorable 1   2   3   4   5   favorable

Sample Reference Check Form_

We would appreciate your appraisal of _____ (SS# _____) who has applied for a position as _____ at [NAME OF CENTER   ].

PLEASE COMPLETE THE INFORMATION BELOW:

Employed by your organization from _____ to _____.

At salary of $ _____ per ☐ hour ☐ week ☐ month ☐ year.

Please check the column that best reflects your assessment of this candidate on the following work-related characteristics:

	Poor	Average	Excellent
Dependability	_____	_____	_____
Initiative and effort	_____	_____	_____
Flexibility	_____	_____	_____
Interactions with children	_____	_____	_____
Interactions with parents	_____	_____	_____
Interactions with co-workers	_____	_____	_____
Professional ethics and conduct	_____	_____	_____
Overall job performance	_____	_____	_____

Would you rehire this individual: Yes _____ No _____

Comments:

Thank you for your assistance. Please sign and date this form below.

Name _____   Position _____

Organization _____   Phone _____

Address _____City _____State _____Zip _____

_____   _____
            signature   date

Staff Orientation Assessment

Please take a few minutes to answer the questions below. Your honest, candid responses will help us continue to meet the needs of new staff in our center.

1. Were you made to feel comfortable and welcome at the center on your first day on the job? Did other staff know you were coming?

2. Were you given enough information about the particulars of our school environment (parking, supplies, storage, lunch routines, schedules, etc.) to help you through those first difficult days?

3. Were you given sufficient background on the center's policies, goals, and philosophy?

4. Were you made to feel that others had a personal interest in your progress? Have other staff made you feel like you are part of the team?

5. Are there any policies or procedures you would like to know more about?

From Bloom, P. J., Sheerer, M., & Britz., J. (1991). Blueprint for action: Achieving center-based change through staff development. Lake Forest, IL: New Horizons. (Assessment Tool #22, pp 246-247). Reprinted with permission.

Available from New Horizons

- *Avoiding Burnout: Strategies for Managing Time, Space, and People in Early Childhood Education* $14.95

- *A Great Place to Work: Improving Conditions for Staff in Young Children's Programs* $6.00

- *Blueprint for Action: Achieving Center-Based Change Through Staff Development* $28.95

- *Blueprint for Action: Assessment Tools Packet* $11.95

- *Workshop Essentials: A Guide to Planning and Presenting Dynamic Workshops* $24.95

The Director's Toolbox: A Management Series for Early Childhood Administrators

- *Circle of Influence: Implementing Shared Decision Making and Participative Management* $14.95

- *Making the Most of Meetings: A Practical Guide* $14.95

- *The Right Fit: Recruiting, Selecting, and Orienting Staff* $14.95

- *Leadership in Action* $14.95 *(Available 2003)*

A Trainer's Guide is also available for each topic in the Director's Toolbox Series. Each guide provides step-by-step instructions for planning and presenting a dynamic and informative six-hour workshop. Included are trainers' notes and presentation tips, instructions for conducting learning activities, reproducible handouts, and transparencies. $69.95

To place your order or receive additional information on quantity discounts, contact:

NEW HORIZONS
P.O. Box 863
Lake Forest, Illinois 60045-0863
(847) 295-8131
(847) 295-2968 FAX